PUBLIC
SPEAKING
SUCCESS

OTHER TITLES OF INTEREST FROM
LEARNINGEXPRESS

Algebra Success in 20 Minutes a Day

Biology Success in 20 Minutes a Day

Chemistry Success in 20 Minutes a Day

Earth Science Success in 20 Minutes a Day

Grammar Success in 20 Minutes a Day

Physics Success in 20 Minutes a Day

Practical Math Success in 20 Minutes a Day

Reading Comprehension Success in 20 Minutes a Day

Statistics Success in 20 Minutes a Day

Trigonometry Success in 20 Minutes a Day

Vocabulary and Spelling Success in 20 Minutes a Day

Writing Skills Success in 20 Minutes a Day

PUBLIC SPEAKING SUCCESS
IN 20 MINUTES A DAY

LEARNINGEXPRESS®

NEW YORK

Library of Congress Cataloging-in-Publication Data:

Public speaking success in 20 minutes a day.
      p. cm.
   Includes bibliographical references.
   ISBN-13: 978-1-57685-746-5
   ISBN-10: 1-57685-746-8
   1. Public speaking. I. LearningExpress (Organization) II. Title: Public speaking success in twenty minutes a day.
   PN4129.15.P838 2010
   808.5'1—dc22
                        2010010695

Printed in the United States of America
9 8 7 6 5 4 3 2 1

ISBN-13 978-1-57685-746-5

For more information or to place an order, contact LearningExpress at:
   2 Rector Street
   26th Floor
   New York, NY 10006

Or visit us at:
   www.learnatest.com

CONTENTS ▶

CONTENTS

CONTENTS

INTRODUCTION ▶

Public speaking is a vital skill in any area of success. If you are a student, speaking well in public will enable you to explain your ideas and persuade others to your opinions. If you are pursuing a career—in virtually any field—good speaking skills will enable you to advance far more quickly than your peers.

Perhaps you feel that you're not a gifted speaker, that public speakers are born and not created. But the truth is that you speak publicly all the time; whenever you gather with a group of friends or answer a question in class or explain something to coworkers, you are speaking publicly. Speaking well is a skill, and no skill is gained without practice.

This book will help you increase your skills as a public speaker. Over the course of the next 20 lessons, you will learn how to be a good listener, analyze your audience, do research, organize your thoughts and notes, prepare an outline, and craft a memorable speech. You will also learn how to use stage fright to your advantage, how to control the audience's responses, how to use visual aids, how to use language, and much more! Use the lined pages in the back of the book to take important notes as you make your way through the lessons.

Each lesson also presents exercises that will help you hone what you've learned, one step at a time. The final lesson presents the texts of several famous speeches so that you can read for yourself how to craft a great speech. All types of speeches are covered: speeches to persuade, to demonstrate, to inform, and to honor special occasions. With this book, some practice, and just 20 minutes a day, you can become a skillful public speaker!

PUBLIC
SPEAKING
SUCCESS

1 ▶ PREPARING TO SPEAK PUBLICLY

Speech is power: speech is to persuade, to convert, to compel.
It is to bring another out of his bad sense into your good sense.
—RALPH WALDO EMERSON, 1803–1882

LESSON SUMMARY

In this lesson, we will consider the most important element of your upcoming speech: the audience. We will also consider several other factors, such as the setting where you'll be speaking.

Before you get up in front of an audience to give a speech, you must first answer these two fundamental questions: *Who am I speaking to? Why am I speaking to them?* The answer to these questions will determine everything about your upcoming speech, including preparation, content, and delivery.

Perhaps you are making a public speech because you are a student in a public speaking class. If that is the case, then your reason for speaking is that you want to succeed as a student. This situation will also define who your audience is: the other students in your class and the professor who is teaching you. Clearly, in this situation, you will want your speech to please the professor, since your final grade will depend upon your performance. However, don't let your desire for a good grade stymie your individual expression. If you follow the advice in this book on crafting and delivering a good, true, and powerful speech, your skills will shine through and you will get the grade you deserve.

Perhaps you are getting ready to speak publicly because you have been asked to do so—making a toast at a friend's wedding, or addressing the members of a church or civic group of which you're a member. Once again, your audience will be clearly defined: the bride, groom, and guests at the wedding, or your fellow members of the church or organization. And once again, you will want your speech to be well received by your audience—you will want to encourage the wedding party or connect with your fellow members on a topic that is of mutual interest.

As you can see, answering the *who* and *why* questions also answers a number of secondary questions:

- What is an appropriate topic?
- How long should you speak?
- What tone should you set?

Each of these questions also needs to be answered, which you will see as we go along, but the first and most fundamental questions are *who* and *why*. Understanding your own motivation for speaking publicly will help you to work through the anxiety that is natural to experience when getting up in front of an audience, and knowing who will be listening will help you anticipate their response. When you feel anxious about your speech, you will be able to focus all that nervous energy on why you are putting yourself through such an ordeal, and use it to your benefit.

Dealing with Anxiety

As you begin preparing to speak publicly, it is also important to know another fundamental fact: Everyone gets nervous about speaking publicly! In fact, most people list public speaking as one of their biggest fears in life, even people who do it professionally. You've probably seen speeches made by people who do it on a regular basis, such as politicians, and thought that they were perfectly poised and not the least bit nervous. But if you were to ask those people if they'd been nervous beforehand, they would quickly assure you that they'd experienced all the butterflies and jitters that you're feeling about your upcoming speech.

We will deal more fully in Lesson 16 with the techniques you can use to turn anxiety into an asset, but for now it's only important for you to know that anxiety is completely normal. The best way to deal with it is to use the energy of your anxiety to produce a good speech—and then you'll have nothing to be anxious about. The first steps to producing a good speech involve laying a solid foundation for it by analyzing who will be in the audience, deciding what you'll be discussing, and visualizing the actual setting of the event.

Who Will Be in the Audience?

At this point in your speechmaking, you may feel as though your public speaking engagement is going to be centered on you. After all, you'll be the one standing up in the front, and you'll be the one doing all the talking. But the truth is that your speech will *not* be centered around you; you will not be speaking for your own benefit, but for the benefit of your audience. It seems incongruous, but public speaking is an art that is centered on the audience, not on the person giving the speech.

Therefore, it will be important for you to know who will be in the audience when you give your talk. Returning to our previous example, if your speech is to be part of a college class on public speaking, your audience will consist of your fellow classmates and your teacher, and it will be in your best interests to tailor your speech to that audience—since at least one member of the audience will be grading your performance!

Analyzing your audience is usually a fairly simple procedure. If you're speaking to a church or civic group, for example, you are probably already a member of that group and know many of the people in the audience. Even if you have been invited to speak to a group of which you are not a member, you can still gain some basic information on the audience by learning what draws them together. A medical conference will probably be attended by medical professionals, for example, and what draws them together is their mutual interest in medical and health issues. You could safely conclude that such an audience would be filled with well-educated professionals, and they would most likely be interested in a speech that addressed some aspect of health and medicine. A civic group such as the local Lions Club or Rotary Club will be made up of a more diverse audience in terms of education and professional background, but they will all be drawn together in a common interest of serving the local community. In that case, you would want to address a topic related to community service.

If you should find yourself speaking to an audience with whom you are completely unfamiliar, you will need to do a little research before beginning your speech. Here are some methods that will help you gain information:

- Ask the person who invited you for detailed information on the audience. That person obviously feels you have something to share that will interest the audience; find out what it is.
- Spend time talking with some individuals who will be in the audience. Ask them for one or two other contacts with whom you can also speak, and ask them what they would be most interested in hearing about.
- Read about the organization on their website or in their brochures or marketing materials.
- Use the Internet to gain background information on the individuals who will be in the audience and on the organization as a whole.
- Visit whatever venue draws the group together. For example, attend a club meeting or event; if it's a group of local merchants, such as the Chamber of Commerce, visit some of the local businesses that are members. Become familiar with the group's area(s) of common interest.

Once you have gained some insight into the audience, you will need to gather some basic information on the meeting at which you will be speaking. Here are some things you will need to know:

- Where will the meeting take place? (This question is important, and we will address it further in this chapter.)
- How large will the audience be?
- What will be the purpose of this meeting?
- What will the audience expect to hear from those who are speaking?
- Will there be other people speaking besides you? If so, where will your speech come in the agenda?
- How long should your speech be?
- How much will the audience already know about your topic? Will you be speaking to experts in the field, or introducing some new topic with which they are unfamiliar?
- What is the age range of the audience? Will you be speaking to a group of high-school students, to senior citizens, or to a wide mix of ages?
- Will your topic be something with which the audience will be in agreement, or might they be somewhat hostile to your ideas?

As you can see, knowing details about your audience will determine a great deal about the speech you write. In this sense, the audience largely determines what you will say, before you have even started writing your speech! A person could be invited to speak on quantum physics to a group of high-school students, but that speech would be vastly different if it were given to a group of rocket scientists. That's because public speaking is entirely focused on the audience, not on the speaker.

Exercise

Fill out this questionnaire before speaking publicly:

■ How many people will be in the audience?

_____

_____

■ What do these people have in common?

_____

_____

■ What is their age range?

_____

_____

■ What is the occasion at which I'll be speaking?

_____

_____

■ How much time will I have?

_____

_____

■ Who is my contact person? How can I reach that person with questions?

_____

_____

Choosing a Topic

It is possible that your topic has been selected for you, perhaps by your professor or by the person who invited you to speak. But it is far more likely that you have been given a good deal of latitude in choosing what you'll speak about, and even if the topic was assigned to you, you still have a good deal of freedom in choosing how you will address it.

Choosing and narrowing a topic can seem like a daunting task at first, but it is actually fairly simple. The first rule is to choose a topic with which you are very familiar. For example, if you are an avid photographer, then photography would be a natural topic for you to choose. If you have been assigned a topic with which you are not at all familiar, then the natural approach is to speak on what it's like to be a beginner in that field. A person who knows little about photography would naturally want to speak on what it's like to be a beginner in the modern field of digital photography—what you've learned about selecting a camera or what useful resources you've discovered on the Internet. Even if you were a beginner in photography speaking to an audience of professionals, your approach to the topic would be fresh and unique, and the audience would undoubtedly enjoy hearing a familiar topic addressed from an "outsider's" perspective.

Here is an age-old maxim in the field of public speaking: "Speak to your strengths." In other words, choose a topic that you know a lot about (assuming that you have that option), because you will naturally have something interesting to say about those things that are of interest to you personally.

This rule applies to every type of speech, whether you are giving a persuasive speech designed to change the audience's opinion on a topic, or making a toast at a friend's wedding. You cannot hope to persuade an audience to your opinion if you don't first *have* an opinion, just as the most memorable toasts are those that display an intimate knowledge of the bride or groom.

Choosing a topic that you know about is not hard, but here are a few ideas to get your creative juices flowing:

- How I chose my major in college
- Why I vote the way I do
- The fun and merits of my favorite hobby
- A person who influenced me greatly in my childhood
- How to . . . (change your oil; get married; raise a puppy; etc.)
- How *not* to . . . (similar to "how to," but with a humorous approach that emphasizes your own personal failures and lessons)
- The history of . . . (your town; your political party; the group that you're addressing; etc.)
- The future of . . . (related to "the history of," but with a greater focus on your thoughts for the future)
- My favorite . . . (book; movie; teacher; ethnic food; or something else that gets you excited)

Once you have chosen your topic, you will find yourself back at our initial premise in this chapter: Ultimately, the audience will determine what you say. You will need to narrow your topic to suit the audience's needs, creating a speech that can be given within time constraints and which addresses something about your topic that will be of interest to the audience.

Let's say that you choose the topic "my experiences in middle school." If your audience is composed of middle-school students, you might speak on "how to make the most of your middle-school years." If your audience is composed of senior citizens, on the other hand, you might speak on "the golden years of middle school." If you are speaking to the local Lions Club, you might speak on "meeting the diverse needs of middle-school students."

The setting and time constraints will also influence your choice of topic. If you have 60 minutes to speak, you could wax eloquent on your reminiscences of those turbulent years in seventh and eighth grade. If you have only 30 minutes, you might narrow the topic to "my favorite teacher in middle school, and how he changed my life." If you have only five minutes, you might narrow it still further and speak on "the one lesson that I learned in middle school."

In each of these examples, you would still be speaking on a topic that you know and love, but you would be narrowing that topic to meet the specific needs of your audience. The main rule to remember is this: Speak about what you know! Keep in mind, however, that even speaking about what you know means you have to do research or talk to experts who might know more than you in order to make a full and robust speech.

Exercise

Fill out this questionnaire before choosing a topic:

- Why was I chosen to speak at this gathering?

_____

_____

- What knowledge do I have that will be of interest to the audience?

_____

_____

- How much will the audience know about this topic?

_____

_____

- How will the audience respond to my views on this topic?

_____

_____

- What type of speech will I deliver? (persuasive, informative, humorous, etc.)

_____

_____

What Will Be the Setting?

The setting of your speech will have an impact upon how your audience responds to your speech. For example, if you are speaking at a banquet immediately after a big meal, your audience will be inclined to doze off. Uncomfortable chairs can make your audience fidgety, while extraneous noise from background music or a nearby party will make it hard for them to pay attention. We refer to such environmental problems as a *hostile setting* for a speaker. It is not that the audience is hostile; it is the environment of the room which makes it difficult for the audience to pay attention. In this case, passion and belief in yourself and your topic are critical. Have confidence in your unique approach and expression of your topic.

You may not have much control over the setting in which you'll be speaking, but knowing what to look for in advance can prepare you to deal with what you're given—and may very well enable you to correct a problem before you speak. Here are a few things that can create a hostile setting:

- The room is too warm or too cold: Too warm makes people drowsy, while too cold makes them fidget.
- Extraneous noise: This can come from external sources over which you have no control, such as a busy highway nearby, or from internal sources which you can control, such as background music being played in a banquet hall. Noise competes with your speech, so treat it as an unwelcome competitor.
- Seating arrangements: Ideally, you want everyone in the audience to be able to see you and hear you easily and clearly. You may find yourself, however, speaking to people who are not ideally situated, such as in a dinner setting where half the audience is facing in the wrong direction across their dinner tables. Using visual aids in that setting would be an excellent idea, since it would force everyone to turn and face you while you speak.
- Lighting: A room that is too dark makes it difficult to see you, while lights that are too bright can be distracting and irritating to the audience. If necessary, turn off some of the lights before the audience arrives, or consider asking for a different location if it's too dark. Also, avoid speaking with a window behind you.

If you are able to control any of these environmental factors, you will be eliminating competitors and giving yourself extra advantages. If you cannot control the environment, you can still give yourself an edge by knowing what the setting is in advance.

Therefore, you should always visit the place where you'll be speaking prior to the day of your speech. This enables you to visualize yourself giving the speech, which helps greatly with anxiety. (We will discuss this further in Lesson 17.) It also gives you an opportunity to correct any problems that are within your control, while also allowing you to anticipate any hostile environment that can't be changed. If you anticipate problems holding your audience's attention, you will want to plan in advance to have visual aids, for example.

Finally, visiting the setting ahead of time also allows you to plan out the mechanics. You can find out where plugs are located for your overheads or slide projection, find out what kind of microphone is (or is not) available, anticipate the seating arrangements that you'll be given, and so forth. Remember the old saying: "Forewarned is fore-armed." When you are aware of problems in advance, you can take steps to overcome them.

Exercise

Fill out this questionnaire while visiting the site of your upcoming speech:

■ What will be the seating arrangements? Will I have any control over this?

_____

_____

■ What is the lighting like? Will I have any control over this?

_____

_____

■ What visual aids will I be using? What will I need to use them? (screen, plugs, projector, etc.)

_____

_____

■ What hostile environmental factors will I be facing? (after dinner, extraneous noise, etc.) What control will I have over these factors?

_____

_____

■ Where will I stand when I speak? Where will I be seated beforehand? How will I walk up to the podium?

_____

_____

TIPS

- Know *who* and *why* before you begin: Who will be your audience? Why are you speaking to them?

- If you don't know your audience, interview your contact person—and ask for other names and phone numbers of people with whom you can talk.

- Talk about what you know. Speak to your strengths. Your audience will respect your words if they sense that you know what you're talking about.

- Visit the place where you'll be speaking prior to the day of your speech. Practice walking to the podium so that you'll be comfortable when it comes time.

- Plan for your needs in advance. Know what equipment or visual aids you'll require, and know where to get what you don't have.

GOOD SPEAKING REQUIRES GOOD LISTENING

It is the province of knowledge to speak and it is the privilege of wisdom to listen.

—OLIVER WENDELL HOLMES, 1809–1894

LESSON SUMMARY

Before you can become an effective speaker, you must learn to be an active listener and observer of your surroundings and your audience. By listening to others and to yourself, you will learn what makes or breaks a great speech.

A wise man once said, "Nobody ever learned anything while he was talking." This is not entirely true when it comes to public speaking, because the art of public speaking can only be learned by speaking in public. In this sense, you *will* learn while you are talking.

Nevertheless, there is still truth in that maxim. You are reading this book because you want to learn how to speak in public effectively, and part of your learning will involve listening. You will want to listen to others who speak well so that you can learn by imitating their styles and content. You will also want to listen to public speakers who *don't* make such a good impression, and learn how to strengthen your own abilities by avoiding their short-comings. Perhaps most important of all, you will want to listen to yourself as though you were sitting in the audience, asking yourself how you'd respond if you were listening to someone else deliver your speech.

This lesson will help you learn how to listen by showing you the sort of problems that can hinder your own public speaking. You will learn these things by paying attention to others who speak in public, whether you're listening to a college lecture or watching a political speech on television, noting the speaker's delivery style and content while also paying attention to how well you're paying attention. You can then take that information and apply it to your own content and delivery, because you will have some understanding of how well your own audience is paying attention to you.

Limited Attention Span

It's a well-known fact that people have fairly short attention spans when it comes to listening to someone lecture. This means that the average audience member can only focus on a speaker's words for a certain period of time before he or she stops listening. The average adult can pay careful attention to a task for approximately 20 minutes before losing focus, and the average length of time for children is much shorter. Modern technology and entertainment, such as television and the Internet, also influence our attention span, and many researchers have suggested that people today have shorter attention spans than people did 100 years ago.

The next time you're listening to someone speak, focus on how well you pay attention. When you catch your mind wandering from the speaker's words, take note of how long you'd been paying close attention before you lost focus. Then bring your mind back to the speaker, and see how long you last before your mind wanders again. If you're like most people, you will find that you last approximately three minutes at a stretch before your attention is diverted.

Also, take note of *why* you stopped paying attention. It doesn't mean you were being disrespectful and it doesn't even necessarily mean that the person giving the speech was doing a bad job. It's human nature to wander.

This knowledge will help you plan your own speeches, since you can generally assume that your audience will be following closely for three minutes before they start to drift away. What you'll want to do is to regain their attention periodically, and you'll want to make the most of those three minutes. We will

discuss some strategies that will help in these areas as we go along.

External Distractions

Simple daydreaming is not the only hazard to an audience's attention span. There can be any variety of environmental factors that distract your listeners, as we discussed in Lesson 1. You might get up at your friend's wedding to offer a toast to the groom, only to have a loud party kick into overdrive in an adjoining room at the banquet facility. You might have a positively brilliant speech planned for your public speaking class, only to arrive and find that the room is overheated and everyone has just finished a heavy lunch.

Some of these factors can be minimized by you, as we discussed previously, but you can generally anticipate that something unexpected will come along to offer distractions to your audience. Just remember this important point: If you have encountered such situations, so has everyone else who speaks publicly. You can learn from this by paying attention to your environment the next time you're listening to someone speak publicly.

First, take note of the environmental factors that are trying to distract you. Perhaps you're seated near two students who are whispering to one another, or maybe there is something fascinating happening outside the windows. Maybe you'll be listening to someone speak after you've eaten a good meal, or maybe you'll be sitting under an air-conditioning vent that is creating icicles down your spine. Whatever the distractions may be, ask yourself what would help you to pay close attention to the speaker—other than removing the source of distraction. Is the speaker aware of the problem? And if so, does he or she overcome it in some way or just continue to drone on? Does the speaker manage to engage your attention despite the distractions? And if so, how? By making light of the situation and then moving on? By upstaging it in a certain way?

You will discover that part of what makes the distraction so distracting is that you *choose* to focus on it rather than on the speaker. Those whispering students draw your attention from the speaker because you choose to listen in their direction rather than toward the person speaking. Perhaps you're dying to know what they're whispering about, or perhaps you simply find the noise irritating. Whatever your reason, the real issue is that you find the whispering more interesting than what the speaker is saying.

This provides you with a very important piece of information: Your audience will be far more likely to pay close attention to your speech if they are interested in what you're saying. Many famous speeches have been given under adverse conditions, yet the audience didn't seem to notice those conditions because they were riveted by what the speaker was saying. For example, both Abraham Lincoln's "Gettysburg Address" and Martin Luther King's "I Have a Dream" were delivered outdoors to large crowds with infinite environmental distractions. King gave his speech at the Lincoln Memorial in the heart of Washington, D.C., with all its traffic and city noise going on all around, while Lincoln delivered his address on a foggy battlefield without the aid of microphone or even a podium.

When you are the speaker, you can take note of the environment even before you get up to the podium, asking yourself what factors might become a distraction to the audience. If there is loud noise coming in the windows, you will remember to speak loudly and clearly to overcome it. If the room is overheated, you will consciously add more animation to your delivery, using large gestures and perhaps walking away from the podium once or twice. If you feel comfortable, you can address the noise or the heat early on, so your audience is aware that you know they might be uncomfortable, and that it matters to you. These techniques will help you to draw the audience's attention away from the distraction and toward your words. And of course, you will know you have written a speech that will be of genuine interest to your listeners, because you spent

time doing your research on the audience before you even began writing.

What's Bugging You?

The central point in this lesson is that you can learn how to be an effective speaker by first becoming an effective audience. If you find something distracting, chances are that others around you are also being distracted by it. At that point, take note of how the speaker handles the situation, and also take note of anything that causes you to pay closer attention to the speaker rather than to the distraction.

In the same way, you will occasionally hear a speaker who simply fails to grab your attention, even though the environment was perfectly suited to his or her talk. That will give you an excellent opportunity to analyze what factors make a speech less effective, and you will know what to avoid in your own speeches in the future. The following sections offer some practical advice on things to cultivate, as well as things to avoid.

The TMI Problem

One of the most common problems with speeches is TMI: too much information. This is actually the downside to the principle that we outlined in Lesson 1: You should always speak about something you know. When you know a great deal about your topic, your natural temptation will be to cram everything into your 20-minute presentation.

The problem with this goes back to our three-minute attention span. If you ask your audience to pay close attention while you pour out a torrent of facts and figures, they will be mentally fatigued by trying to absorb all those facts in a three-minute period, after which they will need to rest their minds by thinking about something else.

Think of your speech as though it were a gun. You could use a shotgun, which fires countless small bullets that scatter in all directions or you could use a rifle, which fires one bullet that penetrates very deeply. In other words, it is better to focus on one or two major points and delve into them deeply than to cover a host of facts in a superficial manner.

We will address these techniques in a later lesson, but it will be helpful here to know how to break up your speech to avoid the TMI syndrome. You can cover a few major points in greater depth, for example, if you provide lots of examples on each point, helping your audience to better understand your ideas by showing them how those ideas work out in a variety of practical situations. This will engage your listeners' minds as they visualize a variety of examples, and it will prevent information overload.

You can also use personal anecdotes and stories that don't seem to have any connection with your speech—provided that you do make a connection by tying the stories back into your main points in some way. This is an effective method of introducing humor into your speech, as well. You can interject a humorous story about something that happened to you when you were in elementary school, and then explain how that experience illustrates your point.

And don't forget about visual aids! Using PowerPoint slides, flip charts, or overhead transparencies will definitely keep your audience awake, because it provides them with something interesting to look at while they also listen to your words. Holding up some object that ties in with your points will keep all eyes riveted on you, and it will prevent information overload by forcing you to make practical applications as you go along.

Make Eye Contact

An important element of being a good listener is to look at the person who is speaking to you. We all know this instinctively; we can all tell when someone isn't listening to what we're saying by watching his or her eyes. Wandering eyes indicate that your listener is more interested in what's going on behind you; blinking eyes may indicate that your listener is confused; squinting eyes can mean that you have angered the other person. But when your listener is looking intently into your eyes, you know that you have his or her full attention.

The same principle works in reverse. If you see that your listener's eyes are wandering, you can regain his or her full attention by moving in front of the person and looking directly into his or her eyes. This brings your listener's attention back to what you are saying, and frequently elicits a response.

When you are speaking to a group of people, you can hold their attention if you make direct eye contact with them as individuals. This also forces you to remember that you are in fact speaking to individuals rather than to an abstract nameless mob. Your audience will find it much easier to pay attention to your speech when you connect with them individually in this way, because it holds each person accountable to listen.

Spice Up Your Speech— Carefully

What is your favorite type of ethnic food? Do you like spicy foods, such as hot chili, or do you prefer more bland foods such as rice or plain noodles? Most meals are made more enjoyable with a little spice—but too much spice can ruin good food.

The same principle is true with public speaking. You can spice up your speech by using visual aids, but too many visual aids can become very distracting. Here are a few techniques that you can use to add some zest to your speech:

- **Visual aids:** As discussed previously, visual aids can add great impact to your speech by demonstrating visually what you are discussing verbally. They also help to keep your audience awake.
- **Humor:** An amusing anecdote from time to time livens up your speech and can also increase your rapport with the audience. Too much humor, however, can backfire, making

you seem like a stand-up comedian rather than someone with a serious message.

- **Practical examples:** It is important to give practical examples in your speech, especially if they address technical matters. But don't get carried away with these, or the audience will think you're treating them like children.
- **Speed bumps:** You can use verbal techniques to jar your audience into attention, such as an unexpected pause or attention-getting phrase like "Now listen carefully to what I'm about to say," or "Did you catch that?" Overuse of such techniques, however, can make you appear too slick.
- **Poetry:** Reciting a short poem is an excellent way to regain your audience's attention, and it can also help them remember your main points. Restrict yourself to one poem per speech, however, which should be just enough to keep it interesting without going overboard.

When the Messenger Hinders the Message

You have probably encountered speakers who have odd mannerisms. I once had a math teacher who would stop lecturing, walk to the window, and stare outside every time a fire engine went past. This peculiar habit may have been endearing, but it was also very distracting—since my high school was located across the street from the fire department. It was a daily affair for his lectures to be interrupted in this way, and each time he had trouble remembering where he'd left off.

Now, most of us are not as eccentric as my math teacher, yet we probably do have some mannerisms and verbal habits that can be distracting to an audience. Frequently, we are not even aware of such mannerisms ourselves. This is one reason why it will be important for you to make a video of yourself giving a speech, which we will discuss in Lesson 17.

Personal mannerisms that can be distracting include rocking back and forth while you speak, playing with your hair or touching your face, sniffling or clearing your throat out of nervousness, or jingling change in your pocket. Verbal mannerisms can also be distracting, such as saying "like" or "you know" frequently, constantly using "um" and "ah" as you search for the right words, or speaking in monotone.

Facial expressions can also work against you, conveying some meaning to the audience that goes beyond your spoken words. If you gaze up at the ceiling, for example, it communicates to the audience that you are confused and uncertain about what you're saying. If you lean forward and jab your finger at the audience, it suggests that you are angry and confrontational—even if you're only speaking about the weather. You might have a smirk without even being aware of it, but it tells the audience that you hold them in contempt.

A speaker's unconscious mannerisms can get very much in the way of what he or she is saying; conversely, they can also be used to great effect to make the message more powerful and memorable. Once again, you can learn a great deal about how body language helps and hinders by paying attention to others who are speaking. What gestures helped this speaker get the point across? What unconscious habits got in the way of that speaker's message? What unconscious habits do you have that might be hindering your own speeches? Being an observant listener will help you become a better speaker.

Pushing Their Buttons

Think back on a time when someone offended you with a casual comment. Perhaps someone told a joke that you found offensive, or maybe someone made a general comment about some religious or political group—not realizing that you were a member of that group. How did you react? What emotions surged up inside you? How did those emotions influence your attitude toward that person?

Now imagine if you were speaking to someone who you didn't know well, and you expressed a strong opinion on some topic—only to discover that your new friend held the opposite opinion just as strongly. How would you feel? What effect would your words likely have on your relationship with the other person?

This same principle holds true, and even more so, when we are speaking publicly. If you angrily denounce some principle that your audience holds dear, you will have lost your audience and gained a hostile mob. There is a time and place for such speeches, but it is very unlikely that you will find yourself in such a situation. The vast majority of speaking occasions will require that you gain the audience's sympathy and good will, not that you stir them into an angry frenzy.

Yet this very problem is more common than you might think. Most speakers don't stand up in front with the conscious intention of offending their audience, yet it is surprising how many beginning speakers do just that—inadvertently. This ties back to Lesson 1, where we discussed the importance of understanding your audience. You need to be sensitive to what your audience might find offensive, and you need to avoid any possibility of giving offense if you want to gain their trust and attention.

A less volatile form of this is to use words and terminology incorrectly. You probably won't make your audience angry, but you certainly will lose credibility. For example, if you were speaking to a group of medical professionals, you would want to be sure that you used medical terminology correctly. Confusing a stethoscope with a kaleidoscope might give your audience a chuckle, but it will also cause them to stop listening. The best approach, if you're not completely sure of yourself, is to avoid technical terminology altogether.

The rule of thumb on offending your audience is this: "When in doubt, leave it out." If you're not sure of technical jargon, don't use it. Or, if you want to include it, do your research! Talk to experts, read books, do everything you can to make absolute certain you know what you're saying is true and correct. If you're not intimately familiar with your audience's views on a controversial subject, think about avoiding that subject—usually, offending your audience means losing your audience. However, if you think you might want to address a controversial issue, you definitely can. Think about starting by sharing a pleasant, familiar anecdote, experience, or idea, and then gently persuading your audience to your point of view. There may be times when you want to challenge your audience, which can indeed be thrilling when it works. Always be respectful and sensitive with your mannerisms and words, and you should be fine.

Exercise

Fill out this questionnaire after listening to someone speak:

■ How would you grade this speaker overall? A, B, C, D

_____

_____

■ In two or three sentences, why did the speaker earn that grade?

_____

_____

■ How well did the speaker communicate information? Was there too much, too little, or just enough?

_____

_____

■ What techniques did the speaker use to help you understand his or her main points?

_____

_____

■ How often did you find your mind wandering? What brought you back to full attention?

_____

_____

■ What environmental factors did you find distracting? How did the speaker overcome those factors?

_____

_____

■ What personal mannerisms did the speaker exhibit? What made them distracting to you?

_____

_____

■ How well did the speaker make eye contact? How many times did he or she meet your eyes?

_____

_____

■ How did the speaker spice up the speech? How effective was the spice?

_____

_____

■ Did the messenger hinder the message, or help it? How?

_____

_____

■ Did the speaker address any controversial topics? If so, how did he or she avoid offending the audience?

_____

_____

■ What were the speaker's major points? Why do you remember them—or not?

_____

_____

TIPS

- Most people have an attention span of approximately three minutes.

- Use spice carefully. Too little spice makes your speech bland, while too much leaves a bad taste.

- Speed bumps can keep your audience alert. Try using dramatic gestures once or twice, or call your listeners to attention: "If you remember just one thing from my talk today, remember this. . . ."

- Always make eye contact with individuals in your audience, but don't hold their gaze for more than a few seconds, and then move on to someone else.

- Personal appearance can help or hinder your speech. If the audience is distracted by your loud necktie or revealing blouse, they won't be listening to your words.

- Make sure you know in advance what might offend your audience, and then tread carefully.

3 ▶ ORGANIZING AND SPICING UP YOUR SPEECH

Organizing is what you do before you do something, so that when you do it, it is not all mixed up.

—A. A. MILNE, 1882–1956

LESSON SUMMARY
In the last lesson, you learned about the importance of adding spice to your speech. In this lesson, you will learn about some tools to help you spice up your speech—and how to keep it organized.

Have you ever wanted a certain item such as a tool, but been unable to find it? I recently needed to test an electrical outlet to see if it was working, and I went in search of my circuit tester. This is a tool that I very rarely use, but I thought I knew just where it was. I didn't. After much aggravation and thrashing around, searching the same toolboxes three or four times over, I went to the hardware store and bought another. I finished the home repair and put away my new circuit tester—right next to the old one that I'd been searching for!

Here is another maxim: "If you can't find it when you need it, you don't own it." I did, in fact, own a circuit tester, but I couldn't find it when I needed it and ended up acting as though I *didn't* own it by purchasing a new one. The basic principle here is that you need to be organized if you want to be effective in any endeavor.

This principle most definitely holds true for public speaking, as much as it does for home repairs or any other task. You will find yourself preparing your speech and thinking, "Didn't Mark Twain . . . or somebody . . . say something funny . . . I think it was funny . . . about this topic?" You may be able to recall the gist of the quotation, but you just won't be able to remember the exact wording, the author, or even where you come across it.

If you were well organized, however, you would be able to track down that quotation in a short amount of time, enabling you to use it to spice up your speech. This lesson will help you get organized now, so that you'll be able to find the tools when you need them in the future.

Using a Computer

The computer is the easiest and most efficient tool for collecting material for speeches. You will use it to gather the information in the first place, which we'll discuss in a moment, but you'll also want to use your computer to organize and save those bits of spice.

The beauty of computer storage is that you can very easily index your material by topic. So let's say that you finally track down that Mark Twain quotation, perhaps this one:

To be busy is man's only happiness.

I found this quotation in a book, so my first step would be to type it into my computer using a standard word processing program. But the next step is very important: The quotation needs to be categorized so that I can find it in the future when looking for spice on a particular speech topic. So at this point, you would ask yourself what speech topics this quotation might be useful for.

Obviously, this Twain snippet would be useful if you were speaking on the topic of *happiness*. Likewise, it would be useful on the topic of *hard work*, and conversely on the topic of *overwork* or *stress management*. It might seem odd at this point to worry about what topics this quotation applies to since it's the only quotation that we've gathered so far. But it will become very important as time goes along, because you will quickly develop the habit of collecting material like this, and as your collection gets bigger, finding material will get much harder.

There are many ways to gather and categorize material like this Twain quotation. If you're fairly savvy with your computer, the best way is to create a database file, since the computer database programs work exactly like the old-fashioned index card system, which we'll consider next. A database file will allow you to categorize each quotation by author and by topic, and it will enable you to easily assign several topics to one quotation.

I use a database that I designed myself to keep track of all my quotations. I only had to type in the Twain quotation once, then I used a series of drop-down boxes to select the topics of *Happiness*, *Work*, and *Stress Management*. Here is what that database card looks like:

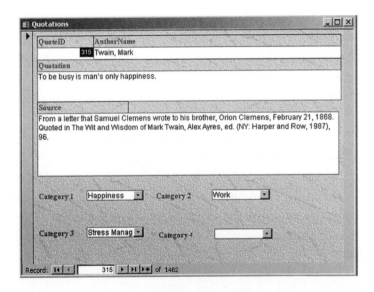

Once you've created a database file, you can easily print out a report of all your quotations listed by topic. Speaking on the topic of gardening? Just open your quotations database file and print out a report of all your quotations on *Gardening*.

However, learning to use a database program can be a daunting task, so if you aren't interested in creating such a file, you can simply create a collection of quotations using a word processing program. Create a category with the header *Happiness*, then type in the Twain quotation below that header. Copy the quotation, create a new header called *Work*, and paste in the Twain quotation there. It's a bit more cumbersome than the database approach, but every bit as effective.

The Old-Fashioned Method

If you don't own a computer, or simply prefer the ease and simplicity of paper, you can choose to organize your quotation files by hand. The simplest of these methods is the 3×5 index card.

Start by purchasing an index card storage box, which will come with alphabetical dividers. You will then fill out an index card something like this:

Happiness

Mark Twain:

To be busy is man's only happiness.

From a letter that Samuel Clemens wrote to his brother, Orion Clemens, February 21, 1868. Quoted in The Wit and Wisdom of Mark Twain, Alex Ayres, ed. (NY: Harper and Row, 1987), 96.

Then you will make another card with the header *Stress Management*, but you won't have to rewrite all the information on that card; simply write "See Happiness: Mark Twain." This will refer you back to the previous card, which you'll have filed in the filing box under the *H* tab.

Finally, you can simply use a standard filing cabinet and create manila folders alphabetically. You could then photocopy and highlight the Twain quotation, filing copies in the *Happiness*, *Work*, and *Stress Management* folders.

Whatever method works best for you, it will be very important that you begin to collect and organize a "spice collection" right away. Following are some tips on how to start your spice collection.

Collecting Your Spice

You will want to spice up your speeches by using pertinent quotations, humorous stories, short pieces of poetry, facts and figures relating to your topic, personal anecdotes, and other such material. This is not a one-time process, however, where you conduct a massive hunting expedition looking for memorable material. On the contrary, this is a habit that you will cultivate and continue throughout your professional career—regardless of what that career happens to be.

Building and maintaining a speech spice file is not like a hunting expedition, it's more like a collecting hobby. Perhaps when you were younger you enjoyed collecting coins or stamps or some other thing. A coin collector is constantly alert for the types of coins that interest him or her, just as a stamp collector will habitually examine every stamp on every envelope that he or she comes across. After a while, it just becomes second nature to scan the change from the cashier or to check the stamps on today's mail.

This is the same habit you will cultivate as you begin to collect useful bits of spice for future speeches. Here are a few sources where you will frequently find what's worth saving.

Regular Reading Habits

Whatever you read on a regular basis, develop the habit of saving anything that might prove useful in a future speech. Your regular reading will be based upon your personal interests, and the basic rule of public speaking is to speak to your strengths. Consequently, your regular reading will be a natural source for speech spice, as it will be on a topic about which you are knowledgeable. This can include:

- newspapers
- news magazines
- trade journals
- fiction and poetry
- technical magazines
- hobby magazines
- religious publications
- textbooks on any topic
- Internet websites

Personal Anecdotes

Any time you find yourself reminiscing about something from the past, jot a note to yourself to add it to your spice collection. You don't need to go into great detail on your database or index card entry; just write down enough to jog your memory about the event, and then categorize it appropriately.

Perhaps you once met a famous athlete and had a short conversation. That experience could easily be used in a speech about setting goals or imitating success or whatever topic was pertinent in that short conversation. Just add an entry in your spice file, with the notation "the time I met so-and-so and we talked about thus-and-such." File it under the appropriate categories, and you're done!

Don't limit yourself to your own stories, either. If a friend tells you of a humorous or memorable experience, add that to your spice file. Just remember to note who told you the story and when, so that you can get your citations and details straight in the future.

Jokes and Witticisms

Have you ever started to tell a joke only to forget the punch line or confuse the details? That's a very common experience, and it can be pretty embarrassing. Imagine how embarrassing it would be to mess up a joke in the middle of a speech!

That's why it's good to add humorous jokes and witty comments into your spice file as soon as you can, while the details are fresh in your mind. Jokes and witty word play can be a powerful spice in an otherwise serious speech, and these entries will be very valuable to you in your public speaking. You might want to memorize this funny spice so that you are ready to improvise in case you find yourself needing to fill gaps with something fun and interesting!

One important thing to remember, however, is to avoid anything that might push your audience's hot buttons, as we discussed in Lesson 2. Keep it clean, or keep it out.

Popular Entertainment

An excellent source of spice will come to you from any area of popular entertainment, including:

- movies
- music
- art
- sports
- television
- radio
- advertising
- periodicals

Popular entertainment can be a rich source of spice simply because your audience will be able to connect with your reference. For example, you might refer to a particular scene in a very popular movie that recently came out, tying it in with your topic. Your audience will be familiar with that movie, at least to some extent, and will be quick to see the connection that you are making in your speech.

Song lyrics can also be a good source of short poetry quotations, while advertising slogans frequently say a great deal in a short sentence. The world of professional sports is a fertile source for all sorts of metaphors that can pertain to just about any speech topic. And there's nothing like talk radio or television shows discussing current events to provide you with attention-getting quotations and statistics.

Internet Searches

Finally, when you're actually working on a speech, you can also do some searching on the Internet for spice on that topic. You will be able to find facts and statistics, memorable quotations, entertaining anecdotes, and plenty more to add into your speech. (We will address this topic in more detail in Lesson 4.)

As you can see, the world is full of speech spice. All you have to do is start collecting!

Exercise

Start a spice file today, and make at least one entry each day for the next two weeks. Include the following information on each entry:

- Name of author, artist, film, etc., and where you got the information.
- Full citation if it's from printed or copyrighted material. This will include the author's full name, the title of the work, publisher, publication date, page number, and so forth.
- Full quotation exactly as written or recorded, if the material is copyrighted.
- Date of the conversation, if it's an anecdote, joke, witticism, etc.
- Category to which it's pertinent, with cross-references to other categories if applicable.

TIPS

Remember to use spice sparingly, but use it! Speech spice can include:

- anecdotes
- jokes
- witty comments
- pertinent facts and statistics
- short poetry
- song lyrics
- personal reminiscences

- Make it a daily habit to record anything that might be useful in a future speech. Record it as soon as possible, while the details are fresh in your mind.

- Keep it clean, or keep it out!

- If you can't find it when you need it, you don't own it.

- A good speaker is a good reader first. Expand your reading habits, and you will also expand your spice collection.

4 ▶ DOING YOUR HOMEWORK

If you steal from one author, it's plagiarism. If you steal from two, it's research.

—WILSON MIZNER, 1876–1933[1]

LESSON SUMMARY

Abraham Lincoln wrote the Gettysburg Address on the back of an envelope. The rest of us need to do research first. In this chapter, we'll cover the basics of doing your homework.

Research is a vital part of any speech, regardless of the topic. We've been emphasizing the importance of selecting a topic that you already know something about, but you will still need to do research even on a topic with which you are very familiar. For example, perhaps you are an avid traveler, and you've chosen the topic "How to Plan the Perfect Vacation." Even though you've traveled all over the world, you'll still need to do some research on appropriate destinations that might interest your audience, the range of airfares they might expect, what sort of accommodations will be available to them, what activities they can enjoy while there, and so forth.

This chapter outlines a variety of sources for your information, but it is not exhaustive. Many of these information sources will serve as springboards, bouncing you to some other source as you begin your research.

---

[1] Quoted in Richard O'Connor, *Rogue's Progress: The Fabulous Adventures of Wilson Mizner* (NY: Putnam, 1975), 167.

Taking Notes

In Lesson 6, we will discuss the mechanics of collecting and organizing the information that you'll use in your speech. For now, just concern yourself with gathering information and taking notes. Be specific as you take notes, and always remember to write down where you found that information. For example, if you found some information in a book, you should write down the author, title, publisher, copyright date, and page number for that note. It is vitally important that you be able to go back to that book at a later date and find the information again.

The main rule here is to take copious notes! Anything that grabs your attention in your reading is worth noting down, even if you don't think you'll need it later. Trust me on this: I can't tell you how many times I've sat down to outline a speech or essay and half-remembered something that I'd read that suddenly becomes pertinent. If I failed to jot down a note on that item, I'm forced to retrace my steps looking for it, and that can be immensely frustrating and time-consuming.

The rule here is the opposite of our usual rule: When in doubt, *don't* leave it out! Interesting illustrations, anecdotes, examples, and so forth are worth including in your notes. You don't need to write down the entire quotation; just make a note that will help you find it later. For example, a magazine article might contain some facts and statistics that are interesting but not seemingly pertinent to your topic. Just jot down "statistics on thus and such" in your notes, with the page number where you found them. There's actually a good chance that you will want to find them again later, and this way you'll know where to look.

Using Personal Experience

The best place to begin your research is with yourself. You have already chosen a topic that you know something about, so use your own experience and knowledge to start your note-taking on the topic. Ask yourself what you'd find interesting if you were to hear someone else speak on your topic. Brainstorm for interesting anecdotes and personal experiences that might work as spice in your speech.

You are actually your best source of information on your topic, and you will want to include examples of your own experience in your speech. This will show the audience that you know what you're talking about, giving you greater credibility and encouraging your audience to take an interest in what you have to say.

As you think through your topic, you will focus on two main things: information, anecdotes, and examples to use in your speech; and insight into what you *don't* know. This second bit of information is immensely valuable, as it will help you know what further research you need to do before you start writing. Incidentally, it will also benefit you greatly in the long run, since you will be learning even more about a topic that already interests you. This is one of the real benefits of being a public speaker: The more you speak on a topic, the more of an expert you become in that topic—and the more likely you'll be asked to speak!

Interviewing Other People

As you spend time thinking through your topic, mining yourself for experiences and information, you will probably think of friends and associates who share your interest in that field. This will naturally occur when you discover a gap in your knowledge; you will instinctively think, "I bet Bill would know the answer to that!"

When that happens, get on the phone immediately and tell your friend that you're speaking on a topic of mutual interest. Don't restrict your conversation to simply answering your question, but ask your friend what he or she would focus on if he or she were speaking on that topic. This will invariably bring up some facet of your topic that you hadn't thought of, and you and your friend can then brainstorm on what information you might cover if you touched on that aspect.

You can also interview people who are experts in some aspect of your topic. Let's return to our previous example, "How to Plan the Perfect Vacation." You could call a travel agency and ask to spend a few minutes with a travel agent discussing ideal locations for vacationers on a budget. The travel agent might know someone who conducts tour groups to London or the Holy Land, and you could then set up an interview with that person—and that person might point you to yet another expert to interview.

Be sure, as always, to take notes while speaking to experts and friends. Remember also to note the person's full name and title, plus the date when you spoke. You might also consider recording the interview if you have a small tape or digital recorder. Here are some basic things to remember as you set up interviews with experts:

- Be prepared: Have a series of questions in mind before you even make the interview

appointment. Also, make sure that your questions can't be answered by some simple research. Nobody likes being asked questions that are basic common sense.

- Be courteous: Remember that the person you're interviewing has a busy schedule and has made time for you out of courtesy. Return the favor by being polite and professional.

- Be prompt: Arrive early for your appointment, and get right down to business rather than chatting about unrelated topics. When the interview is completed, thank the expert and leave.

- Be thorough: This interview may be your only opportunity to speak with the expert, so make sure that you understand the information that he or she is sharing. Even if you use a tape recorder, take notes while the expert speaks. Reiterate some of his or her points to ensure that you correctly understood what was said.

Exercise

Use this form to prepare for an interview:

- Interviewee's name, address, and phone number

_____

_____

- Date of interview

_____

_____

- Topic of interview

_____

_____

■ Questions that I'll ask (list out at least five very specific questions)

_____

_____

■ Time and length of appointment (once you've made the initial contact)

_____

_____

Using the Internet Responsibly

The Internet is a good place to start your further research, but bear in mind that it is just that: a place to *start*. You can find a vast array of information on practically any topic simply by typing the topic into a search site such as Google or Yahoo!, and some of the information might be very detailed. The problem is that there is very little accountability for what people post on the Internet. Anyone can create a website and then wax eloquent on any topic whatsoever—regardless of whether or not that person knows anything about that topic.

You will want to use Internet information to gain a broad overview of a topic and to find sources of more detailed and reliable information in books and periodicals. Use the Internet as your first stop, and then plan on heading to the library.

Here are a few good starting points for Internet research:

■ Search sites: Each search site will bring up a slightly different blend of hits on any given search—as well as a good deal of overlap. Try searching for the same topic on Google, Yahoo!, Ask.com, and Answers.com.

■ Encyclopedias: Back before computers, the natural first step in any research was to consult an encyclopedia, usually a multivolume collection such as the *Encyclopedia Britannica*. Today, one's first stop might be an online encyclopedia such as Wikipedia. Bear in mind, however, that entries on such sites can be written by anyone, whether or not that person has any depth of knowledge on the subject. Some other online encyclopedias include *Encyclopedia Britannica* (Britannica.com), *Encyclopedia.com*, *MSN Encarta* (Encarta.MSN.com), and *Library Spot* (LibrarySpot.com).

■ Web rings: A web ring is actually a list of websites that are devoted to any particular topic. If your topic is landscape photography, do a search for "landscape photography web rings" and you'll bring up a long list. (Note that *web ring* can be spelled as one word or two.) Click on a web ring link, and it will bring up a list of links to specific sites on that topic.

■ Online bookstores: An excellent way to find sources of information is to find out what's been written on that topic—and this is a natural precursor to your library visit, as well. You don't need to buy any books; you can simply find out which titles best meet your needs. Some sites to search would include *Amazon, Barnes and Noble, Borders,* and *Abe Books* (AbeBooks.com, specializing in out-of-print books).

- Library online catalogs: Finally, before actually visiting a library, spend some time on an online library catalog. Most states have their public libraries connected in an interlibrary loan program, and most local libraries have a website with a link to the state's library catalog. You can do a search for books by subject, browse through titles, and request that specific books be sent to the library nearest you.

Exercise

Use this form when doing Internet research:

- Name of website

  _____

  _____

- Website's exact Internet address (for simplicity, type this form into your computer, then copy and paste the web addresses to avoid typos)

  _____

  _____

- Date when I looked at the page

  _____

  _____

- Notes on what I learned there

  _____

  _____

- Further references (books, periodicals, reference materials, etc., to which the site refers)

  _____

  _____

Visiting the Library

Your greatest and most reliable source of information will be at your local library. As already mentioned, most states these days have interconnected their local public libraries into a book-sharing system, which means that the entire collection of every library in your state is available to you—without having to travel!

Begin your library research by finding your state's interlibrary loan website, then search through their catalog by subject. You can then request any books be sent to the library nearest you; when you're done with those books, simply return them to the same library. (This process may require that you have a library card at a member library in your state. If you don't already have a library card, *get one!* You'll use it for the rest of your life.)

Next, you'll want to visit your local library in person, because many of their most valuable research tools cannot be taken home. The first and most valuable of these resources is the librarians themselves! These are the people who spend their professional lives immersed in books, and they possess a vast breadth of knowledge. In fact, many larger libraries have personnel who specialize in research, known as research librarians. Ask these experts to point you toward materials on your topic, and you'll save a great deal of time.

Following are some of the vast resources that you'll find at your local library.

Books

Books are the best source of in-depth and detailed information on any topic you can think of. They will cover your topic in far greater detail than any website or periodical, simply because books have more space devoted to the subject than websites or periodicals can conveniently afford.

Another important feature of books is that you (and your audience) can refer to them at a later date. Websites can change or disappear overnight, but that book will be on your library shelves for years to come.

Finally, books will address many aspects of your topic, enabling you to refine your speech. If you want to speak on horses, there will be books available that discuss the care and feeding of horses, how to raise riding horses, how to breed racehorses, the history of domesticated horses, what equipment is used to train horses—and, of course, books on horses in general. Simply browsing along a library shelf can give you valuable ideas on how to narrow your topic.

Periodicals

Periodicals include magazines, trade journals, academic journals, newspapers, and many other publications that come out periodically. These are a valuable resource for information that needs to be up to date. If you're speaking on healthcare issues, for example, you'll certainly want to investigate books on the subject—but you'll also want to consult relevant periodicals to gather some recent facts and statistics.

You'll quickly discover that there is a whole world of periodicals in print, and simply browsing through your library's periodicals section will prove overwhelming. The best method is to consult the library's best resource, as previously discussed: the librarian. This is especially true if your library has a dedicated research librarian, because that person is familiar with the immense selection of periodicals on file, and can quickly direct you to the best sources.

The librarian will also be able to direct you to indexes and search engines that are specifically dedicated to periodicals, known as periodical indexes. These indexes are generally computerized to make search faster and easier. (Your state library might even have a periodical index available on its interlibrary website.) They are up-to-date listings of thousands of periodicals that work just like a library card catalog, permitting you to do a search by subject to find out which issues of what publications had articles on that topic. Some of the most commonly used periodicals indexes are the *Reader's Guide to Periodical Literature*, the *Social Sciences Index*, the *Humanities Index*, and the *Education Index*.

Remember: When in doubt, ask a librarian.

Microfilm and Microfiche

Many periodicals, such as newspapers, make their back issues available in micro-formats. Microfilm and microfiche are miniature photocopies of each page in a periodical, and they utilize special viewing machines that magnify those pages and even allow you to print them out. In this way, libraries can retain newspapers and other periodicals indefinitely, allowing you to read the current events of last century.

This can be especially useful if you want to discuss a certain trend in your speech. Returning to our horses example, you might want to discuss how horse racing has changed in the last 50 years. You might find it useful to consult periodicals from 50 years ago to see what was being written about the subject, and you'd find those periodicals available in microfilm format.

Reference Materials

I mentioned encyclopedias in connection with their modern online equivalents, but those books are still printed today as well. Your local library will be well stocked with an array of reference books that will prove invaluable in your research. Here are just a few examples:

- encyclopedias
- dictionaries
- atlases
- books of quotations
- almanacs
- yearbooks and date books
- indexes and cross-indexes
- government documents

Exercise

Use this form when doing library research:

- Book title:

  _____

  _____

- Author:

  _____

  _____

- Publisher:

  _____

  _____

■ Copyright date:

_____

_____

■ Call number (the number used by the library to find the book):

_____

_____

■ Notes:

_____

_____

TIPS

■ Begin your research inside your own head, brainstorming for anecdotes, personal experiences, and insights that can add spice to your speech.

■ Don't rely solely on Internet research; use your library!

■ When in doubt, ask a librarian.

■ Take notes! You might think that you'll remember what you're reading or that great idea that just came to mind—but you won't. Write it down.

■ Write down complete citations for all research material so that you can refer back to it at a later date.

■ Summarize the main ideas of your research, perhaps at the top of the document, in terms you can quickly reference and understand.

5 ▶ THE MAJOR TYPES OF SPEECHES

Speak properly, and in as few words as you can, but always plainly; for the end of speech is not ostentation, but to be understood.

—WILLIAM PENN, 1644–1718

LESSON SUMMARY

Whatever your reason for speaking, this chapter will help you understand and achieve your goals on any speaking occasion.

As William Penn wisely remarked, the primary goal of any speech is to be understood, not to impress the audience with eloquence. Yet there are secondary goals to one's speech, beyond simple communication. Your secondary goal might be to teach the audience a new skill, or you might want to persuade the audience that one type of toothpaste is better than another, or you might simply want to entertain with warm and funny stories of the bride and groom.

Whatever your speech occasion may be, you will have two goals in mind before you even begin. The first goal is firm and fixed—to communicate and be understood—while the second goal will determine the type of speech you write. There are probably as many types of speech as there are speeches given, in the sense that every speech is unique, but we can categorize most speeches into four groups:

- Informative
- Demonstrative
- Persuasive
- Special Occasions

Informative Speeches

An informative speech is essentially a lecture. It is intended simply to inform your audience on some topic. If you're a student, you hear informative speeches all day long in your classes, as your teachers and professors stand up front and lecture on various subjects. Your teachers are trying to inform you, and their lectures are essentially informative speeches.

Some informative topics you might consider are:

- Current trends in . . .
- The future of . . .
- The history of . . .
- The pleasures of a particular hobby
- Common causes of allergies
- When to buy a home
- Famous explorers and their discoveries
- What equipment is needed for . . . [backpacking, kayaking, carpentry, etc.]

An informative speech is different from a how-to speech or a persuasive speech because it is only intended to provide information. You will leave it up to your audience to decide for themselves what to do with the information; you are not trying to persuade them to think as you do, nor are you specifically teaching them *how* to do something. You are only concerned with providing information for your audience on a particular topic.

Informative speeches are useful as an introduction to some topic that is unfamiliar to your audience. And this is where your audience research pays off, which you learned about in Lesson 1. You will want to be acquainted with what your audience already knows. After all, you wouldn't want to lecture on "The History of the Airplane" to an audience of NASA scientists. On the other hand, you *could* give an informative speech on "The Materials Used by the Wright Brothers for Their First Airplane" to that NASA audience. They might be well versed in the overall history of the airplane, but they might *not* know what exact materials were used at Kitty Hawk.

You will also want to know what topics will be of interest to your audience. Will your listeners care to learn about your favorite hobby, or will they be bored and distracted? The best way of answering this question, if you don't already know your audience, will be to conduct some basic interviews, beginning with the person who invited you to speak.

What to Do

Think about the best teachers you've ever had. Ask yourself what made those teachers so effective. How did they lecture? How did they interact with the students? How did they establish rapport with the students? These questions will help you gain insight into what makes an effective informative speech.

One of the most important things to include in an informative speech is, quite naturally, information. You will want to do research on facts and statistics, ensuring that your speech has something interesting to impart to the audience. Those facts and statistics will probably be best communicated with visual aids, such as charts, graphs, illustrations, and so forth.

Remember, however, to be practical. If you provide extensive information on allergies, for example, your audience will become anxious to know how to *avoid* allergies. Your speech should include some sort of practical application so that your audience will know what to do with the information you've provided. Your favorite teachers probably did this, whether you were aware of it or not. A dull math professor lectures on theory and problem-solving, but an interesting math professor will tell you how to use those theories in real-life situations. Do the same for your audience.

Lectures that are filled with information, however, run the risk of being dull (as we'll mention further in a moment). One way to avoid this danger is to interact with your audience. Your favorite teachers probably knew how to do this effectively, inviting students to answer questions, voice opinions, wrestle with problems, and so forth. Your best approach when giving an informative speech will be to get the audience involved. Here are a few ways to do this:

- Ask questions: You can use this to illustrate that most people have misconceptions on your topic, or to find out what they already know.
- Invite questions: Rather than pushing questions to the end of your talk (which is normally preferable), urge your audience to raise their hands as you go along if a question occurs to them. This helps them pay attention, and helps you to meet their needs.
- Solicit examples: You will want to provide examples and visual aids in your speech, but you can also ask the audience if they've had experience with what you're talking about. This will enrich your speech by providing the audience with more perspectives on the topic, and it will hold their attention.
- Make them apply the information: Remember that you want to provide practical application to your information. An ingenious way of doing this is to ask the audience what *they* will do with the information you've provided. You'll still need to have some practical applications of your own in mind, but they will undoubtedly think of things that you didn't.

What to Avoid

Every rule has its counter-rule, and informative speeches are no exception. We already noted that informative speeches need information, including facts and statistics, but the counter-rule is that too much information will undermine your efforts. Think again about those teachers whom you found boring and dull. It is likely that you've listened to someone drone on, endlessly spouting facts and figures and theories and principles and on and on—and you probably left that lecture feeling like your head was stuffed with cotton.

This is known as information overload (or *TMI*, as discussed in Lesson 2), and it's a common pitfall when giving an informative speech. You have chosen a topic about which you are knowledgeable, and you want to share that knowledge with your audience. But you'll first need to select *what* knowledge you want to share, and this will entail deciding in advance *not* to share other areas of knowledge.

Remember the shotgun analogy used in Lesson 2? A shotgun scatters many little pellets that don't go very deep, while a rifle fires one bullet that penetrates to a great depth. This illustration also applies to informative speeches: it's better to cover a few points in depth than to hit a thousand points on the surface. You don't want too little information in your speech, but you also don't want too much. Decide which information will be interesting to your audience, and focus your energy on that.

You can also overdo some of the techniques for involving the audience, which we discussed earlier. You want to include your listeners in the learning process, but you don't want to make them do your work for you. Always be prepared to answer your own questions, to provide your own applications and examples, and to inform your audience without their help. After all, *you* are the expert on the topic, and that's why you're addressing the audience in the first place.

Demonstrative Speeches

The demonstrative speech is closely related to the informative speech because it centers on providing your audience with information. The main difference, however, is that the demonstrative speech is a "how-to" lecture. Rather than passing on raw information to your listeners, you are teaching them some very practical skills.

The best way to prepare a demonstrative speech is to ask yourself *how* and *why* questions. "How does a computer work?" "Why does ice float?" "How do I buy a new home?" "Why does electricity have positive and negative forces?" You would then answer those questions through a practical demonstration.

For example, if you wanted to explain how a computer works, you'd probably want to use a real-life computer to demonstrate. You'd also want visual aids, such as charts or diagrams, which explain the processes that can't be seen easily by the audience.

The key to a demonstrative speech is to focus on practical application, not on abstract facts and statistics. Your goal is to teach the audience *how to*, not to tell them *what is*—*how to* bake a chocolate cake, not *what is* a chocolate cake. Here are some topic ideas to get you brainstorming:

- How to make something
- How to repair something
- How *not* to make or repair something (using humor to teach *how to*)
- How something works
- How to play an instrument, paint a picture, write a book, raise a pet, etc.
- How to create a budget, save money, build a business, etc.
- How to raise children, choose a school, find a mate, plan a wedding, etc.
- How to read, write, speak a foreign language, etc.

What to Do

Use visual aids! These are helpful in any speech, but they are the very backbone of a demonstrative speech. If you want to tell your audience how to fix a computer, you'll certainly need a computer to demonstrate on. The same holds true for things that are more abstract, such as planning a wedding or learning a language. The visual aids may not be as self-evident as in fixing a computer, but they are still vitally important in helping your audience visualize the practical steps you are teaching.

And practical is what a demonstrative speech is all about. Remember to keep it that way, focusing on *how to* rather than *what is*. Before you begin writing your speech, determine what practical skill you want your audience to gain. Then ask yourself what steps are involved in accomplishing that skill—and you've got the major points of your speech all mapped out.

What to Avoid

Visual aids are critically important to your demonstrative speech, but you must also avoid letting them become a source of distraction. There are two groups who can be distracted by your visual aids: the audience, and *you*!

You want your audience to be paying primary attention to your words and actions, with a secondary focus on your visual aids. Remember that the visual aids are just that: aids. They are not the speaker, they are merely *aiding* the speaker. If you use diagrams and flow charts in your presentation, make sure they contain only what is necessary to illustrate your points. You want your audience to look at them as you speak, but you don't want them to be contemplating your lovely artwork rather than listening to your words.

Conversely, remember that you are speaking to an audience, not to a visual aid. I've seen many speakers who held up an object as an illustration but forgot to show it to the audience! One speaker recently recommended a book on his topic, then spent time looking at the cover of the book rather than showing it to his listeners. If you're telling the audience how to repair computers, don't bury your head inside the computer case and mumble into the hard drive; lift your head to face the audience and simply point to the objects that you're discussing.

As with too many facts in an informative speech, you can have too many visual aids. This will become a distraction to you as you fumble about moving objects around or searching for the right slide, and it will become overwhelming to the audience, leaving them with the same cotton-headed feeling they'd get from information overload.

Persuasive Speeches

The persuasive speech is also related to the informative speech, except that you are doing more than simply providing information on your topic—you are also providing your own opinion on that topic and attempting to persuade your audience that your opinion is correct. And this element of opinion and persuasion is what makes the persuasive speech the most challenging of the four types.

The key to writing a persuasive speech is to begin by having an opinion—preferably an opinion that you feel strongly about. If you have no opinion on a topic, you won't be able to persuade anyone else to hold an opinion. You must first know *what* you believe and *why* you believe it. It isn't enough to say, "I believe that this toothpaste is better than that toothpaste, and I want you to believe it, too." Your audience will immediately ask you *why* you hold that belief.

So before you begin your speech, you must first ask yourself what you believe in strongly, and then ask yourself why you hold that belief. List the reasons why you believe that toothpaste A is better than toothpaste B—because it whitens, eliminates bad breath, and costs less. These reasons will become the major points in your speech with which you explain to your audience *why* toothpaste A is better than toothpaste B.

Aristotle was a Greek philosopher who lived in the fourth century B.C. He outlined the three basic ways in which a speaker can persuade his audience to embrace his beliefs. He used Greek words to describe these methods, but we'll update them into modern concepts as we go. They are:

- **Ethos:** Credibility, image, public reputation, perceived expertise
- **Logos:** Words, concepts, logic
- **Pathos:** Emotions, feelings, gut reactions

First, a persuasive speaker must be a credible speaker, fitting into Aristotle's category of *ethos* or credibility. The audience needs to recognize that you know what you're talking about, and that you are qualified to be telling them the difference between right (your opinion) and wrong (your opponents' opinions). The old adage "practice what you preach" fits into this category. You are not likely to be persuaded to some moral standard by a speaker who doesn't follow that standard him or her self.

Similarly, you must let your audience know two things: that you have the expertise in your topic which qualifies you to hold a strong opinion, and that you make decisions yourself based upon that opinion—decisions which have better results than those to which the opposite opinion would lead.

Second, you must use either strong logic or strong emotional appeals—or both—to persuade your audience that your opinion is the correct one. Having credentials and credibility is not enough; you will need to give your audience a reason to embrace your opinion, and you might need to give them a reason to care about your topic in the first place.

Appealing to Logic

Logic is more difficult to master than emotional appeals, but it is far more effective. You build a logical argument by stating an opinion, then explaining a number of reasons that logically support that opinion, and finally, providing examples of each that illustrate your point and prove that it's true.

Let's use the toothpaste example once more. Here is how you might structure the outline for your persuasive speech, in which you want to persuade your audience that toothpaste A is better than toothpaste B:

Thesis: Toothpaste A is better than toothpaste B.

Point 1: Toothpaste A prevents cavities, while toothpaste B does not.

Illustration: A recent study by the Molar Meddler's Guild demonstrated that toothpaste A provided 82% more cavity coverage than any other brand.

Point 2: Toothpaste A brightens while it cleans, whereas toothpaste B turns teeth green.

Illustration: Visual aids showing closeup photos of teeth brightened by A and made quite colorful by B.

Point 3: Toothpaste A costs less than B.

Illustration: I conducted a personal survey of 12 local pharmacies and grocery stores, and found that, on average, A cost 12 cents less than B.

Conclusion: On every level, toothpaste A is better than toothpaste B.

Notice that you have stated several reasons for your thesis (the opinion you intend to prove to your audience), and have given examples that demonstrate each reason. This approach uses logic (Aristotle's *logos*) to persuade your audience.

Appealing to Emotions

You can also appeal to the emotions of your audience (Aristotle's *pathos*) with an argument that has little basis on logical fact. Here is an outline for such a speech:

Thesis: Toothpaste A is better than toothpaste B.

Point 1: Toothpaste A tastes good, but toothpaste B is yucky.

Illustration: Toothpaste A reminds me of a cool ocean breeze on a hot summer's day, but the last time I tried B, I nearly gagged.

Point 2: Toothpaste A is fun to use, and kids love it.

Illustration: Visual aid showing photos of the colorful stripes in toothpaste A, compared to the muddy brown of toothpaste B.

Point 3: I interviewed more than a dozen people, and they all preferred toothpaste A.

Illustration: Visual aid video showing interesting people describing how much they enjoy brushing with toothpaste A.

Conclusion: On every level, toothpaste A is better than toothpaste B.

As you can see, this outline provides no logical proof that one toothpaste is any better than the other. Your argument might persuade some in the audience to switch toothpastes, but another emotional appeal from another speaker could easily sway them back to a different opinion. The better method is to use both logic *and* emotional appeals to persuade your audience.

What to Do

Remember that your thesis is an opinion, and your opinion must be proven if you want to persuade your audience. It does no good to say, "I like toothpaste A and you should, too!" That will not persuade anybody; you need to give them clear reasons *why* they should embrace your opinion.

When building a logical argument, think of it as though you were a lawyer proving your case in court. Let's say that you want to prove that John Smith murdered Bill Jones. Here's how you would construct your case:

Thesis: John Smith murdered Bill Jones.

Evidence 1: Here is the revolver that he used to shoot him.

Explanation: It has been proven that this gun fired the fatal bullet, and Smith's fingerprints were found on the handle.

Evidence 2: Jones and Smith were seen arguing just before the shooting.

Explanation: Smith was angry with Jones and threatened to kill him, and three witnesses heard him just prior to the gunshots.

Evidence 3: Smith has no alibi for where he was at the time of the shooting.

Explanation: Since Smith was seen by witnesses at the scene just moments before the crime, it is beyond doubt that he committed it.

Conclusion: There is no reasonable doubt that John Smith shot Bill Jones.

This same formula can be applied to any persuasive speech. Remember that your thesis is merely an opinion, and opinions must be accompanied with proof if you want to persuade your audience.

What to Avoid

The danger of logical arguments is that they can become a mere brow-beating in which you hammer your audience over the heads with facts and statistics. Simply repeating your opinion over and over will not convince the audience; you must provide a variety of evidence to support your thesis.

On the other hand, emotional appeals can become repulsive if they are heavy-handed. If your audience detects that you are trying to appeal to their emotions, they will probably react in the opposite direction from what you intended.

Finally, remember the old saying: "It's easier to attract flies with honey than with vinegar." An angry or belligerent attitude will cause your audience to become defensive, and you will have a difficult time persuading them to your opinion. Body language, delivery, word choices—even the very evidence that you present—will all influence how your audience responds to your message. Remember Aristotle's concept of *ethos* or credibility: You want to be perceived as a credible and reliable speaker on your topic, and the best place to start is to appear friendly and approachable while you speak.

Special Occasions

This final category of speechmaking is quite broad and differs significantly from the others. You might be asked to "say a few words" at a special occasion, which could be as little as a one-minute toast or as lengthy as a 30-minute speech. Here are some examples:

- Toasting the bride and groom at a wedding
- Introducing the main speaker at a conference
- Summarizing your project status at a business meeting
- Eulogizing a friend at a funeral
- Presenting or accepting an award at a banquet

There are two subtypes of speeches within this category: the prepared speech, and the impromptu speech.

Making a Prepared Speech at a Special Occasion

If you're warned ahead of time that you'll be called upon to say a few words at some special occasion, you will follow all the same techniques that we've been discussing thus far. You'll want to think about your audience, considering who will be present when you speak and what they'll want to hear you say.

Your topic will be defined for you, to some extent. For example, if your boss wants you to summarize your projects, your topic will be the relevant projects on which you're currently working. If the bride and groom want you to open the wedding banquet with a toast or introductory remarks, your topic will be the happy couple. But what you say on those topics will still be up to you, and you will want to consider setting an appropriate tone.

The tone of a speech is defined as the mood you want to create. Humor is very appropriate at a wedding banquet, while sober thoughts on finances and marital hurdles might be out of place. The opposite is probably true at a business meeting with your boss and coworkers, where the audience is not expecting to be entertained with jokes but wants to hear about financial matters, project problems, expected completion dates, and so forth.

Tone will be as important as topic in most special occasion speeches. Humor is acceptable at a funeral; indeed, it is often very healing to those who are grieving. Yet you also don't want to be flippant, causing the mourners to feel as though you are making light of their grief and loss. Setting the right tone requires that you put yourself in the place of your audience, asking yourself what you would think appropriate or inappropriate if you were in their shoes. If there's any doubt, it's best to remember the famous line from a once-popular TV detective show: "Just the facts, ma'am." Stick to facts, and you won't go wrong.

Making an Impromptu Speech at a Special Occasion

There will be times when someone will ask you to say a few words without advance notice, asking you to stand up right there and then to address the audience. This can seem terribly intimidating, but the same principles apply to an impromptu speech as to any other speech: Consider your audience, and speak about what you know.

This is another instance of the adage, "forewarned is fore-armed." If you are attending a special occasion where you might possibly be asked to speak, give some thought beforehand to what you would say. Better still, it is often good to take the bull by the horns and volunteer to say a few words. This prevents you from being caught off guard, makes you someone's hero who might otherwise have been asked to speak, and gives you practice at becoming a more confident speaker.

When you give a prepared speech, you will probably be working from a written speech or outline, and having your thoughts committed to paper gives you increased confidence. There is no reason for you not to use that same technique in an impromptu speech, even if you only have a few minutes to prepare. Ask yourself what the audience will want to hear, what tone is appropriate, and what basic facts you want to relate—then jot them down on a small piece of paper or napkin or whatever is handy. Having this cheat sheet in your hand or pocket will give you greater confidence as you get up to speak, because you'll already know what you're going to say.

One benefit of being asked to speak spontaneously is that you don't have a lot of time beforehand to get nervous! It also encourages you to be brief and to the point in your speech—which might be the very reason that people do it in the first place. Just remember that one of the most famous speeches in American history, Abraham Lincoln's *Gettysburg Address*, was very short and succinct, lasting only three minutes. You can move your audience just as effectively with a few words as you can with a lengthy prepared speech, so it's a good idea to keep impromptu words to a minimum.

What to Do

When making a speech at a special occasion, whether prepared or impromptu, the most important things are to be appropriate and stay focused. Remember that the whole reason for speaking is the occasion itself, so your thoughts should always remain centered on that occasion.

If you're speaking at a graduation ceremony, you'll probably be given at least 15 minutes in which to speak—but that is not an excuse to ramble around in your thoughts on a variety of topics. Most special occasion speeches will be shorter simply because the occasion calls for other activities besides listening to a speech. That's the point of special occasion speeches: Nobody came to the gathering in order to hear a speech, unlike other forums where you might be asked to speak. The audience is gathered to recognize a person or event, and you do not want your speech to interfere with that.

You will also want to speak clearly and loudly, topics that we'll discuss in detail in Lesson 13. On many special occasions, you will not have the luxury of a microphone or even visual aids. Your audience might be standing around in a drizzle by a grave side, or you might be addressing coworkers from the middle of a crowded hotel meeting room. You will want to be sure that everyone can hear you clearly and that everyone can see your face. If necessary, move to a prominent position, such as the front of the room or on a high point of land, so that everyone can see you and hear you.

What to Avoid

Be brief! As already mentioned, the audience has not gathered specifically to hear your speech. On most special occasions, your audience will welcome a few brief words from someone who has special knowledge about the person or event being commemorated, but the key word there is *brief*. As already stated, stay focused on your topic and keep your thoughts from rambling.

Avoid using humor that is inappropriate. This rule applies to all speeches, of course, but it can become a real pitfall in special occasion speeches simply because the special occasion may be a happy, family-oriented celebration of some sort, such as a birthday or wedding. There will be an atmosphere of joking and laughter in the air, and it can be tempting to let fly with some real zingers—especially if the audience is already predisposed to laugh at your witticisms. But there is always a fine line at any gathering between appropriate teasing and inappropriate or coarse jesting, and there is nothing worse for a public speaker than expecting a guffaw from the audience but getting a stunned silence instead. Remember our golden rule: When in doubt, leave it out!

Do not drink alcohol if you think you might be asked to speak. Again, this rule applies to all speech situations, but some special occasions may provide a much greater opportunity to forget the rule. Among the many adverse effects of alcohol is its effect on your ability to speak clearly. Just one drink can add a perceptible slur to your speech, even if you haven't overindulged. Alcohol is also notorious for bad judgment, and something that seems appropriate after a couple drinks will make you cringe in shame the next morning. Simply put, speaking and drinking don't mix.

Exercise

Use this questionnaire to determine the direction of your speech:

1. What is my goal in this speech?
   - ❏ Inform my audience (go to question 2)
   - ❏ Persuade my audience (go to question 3)
   - ❏ Teach my audience some skill (go to question 4)
   - ❏ Commemorate a special event (go to question 5)
2. What facts do I want them to know? What will I need (visual aids, etc.) to convey those facts? (After filling in this information, go to question 6.)
3. What opinion do I want to prove? What points of evidence will I provide? How will that evidence prove my thesis? (After filling in this information, go to question 6.)
4. How exactly is this skill performed or learned? What steps are taken to accomplish it? What visual aids will I need to teach those steps? (After filling in this information, go to question 6.)
5. Who or what is the reason my audience will be gathering? What facts do I want to discuss concerning that person or event? What anecdotes will I include?
6. What research is needed? What information do I *not* know?

TIPS

- Persuasive speeches provide an opinion that must be proven. If you don't prove your opinion, you won't persuade your audience.

- Informative speeches can become very dull if they're too crammed with facts. Restrict yourself to a few facts and cover them thoroughly.

- How-to speeches can be very interesting and entertaining for both audience and speaker. Just remember that *you* are the center of attention, not your visual aids.

- Never mix alcohol with public speaking.

- Whatever your special occasion, remember that the audience is *not* there to hear you speak.

LESSON

6 ▶ PREPARING AN OUTLINE

The beginning of an acquaintance whether with persons or things is to get a definite outline of our ignorance.

—GEORGE ELIOT, 1819–1880

LESSON SUMMARY

Before you can begin writing your speech, you must make an outline. This is like the roadmap of your speech, showing you your destination and how you'll get there.

No matter what type of speech you make, regardless of the occasion, and no matter how you deliver it—you will want to start with an outline! The outline is the skeleton on which you will build a living speech, and it will determine exactly what that speech will look like and what it will accomplish.

There are several important things that you'll gain by creating a preliminary outline. First, you'll discover what you know—and what you *don't* know. A person never knows how much he or she knows until he or she tries to explain it to someone else. You won't know how much knowledge you really have about your topic until you sit down and outline a speech on that topic.

Another benefit of outlining is that it enables you to accomplish your goal. If you're making a persuasive speech, the outline will force you to specify what your sub-points are (the *evidence* that proves your thesis), what examples you'll provide for each sub-point, how the sub-points prove your thesis, and so forth.

You probably would not dream of getting up at the podium on the day of your speech and just making it up as you go along; that would lead to disaster, and you would fail to accomplish whatever goal you were trying to achieve. Yet the same principle holds true if you sit down to write a speech without first creating an outline: You'll simply be making it up as you go along without any clear sense of where you're going and how you'll get there.

Hit the Target

If you were engaged in archery practice, what would be the first thing you'd do? You might check your arrow supply, test the bowstring, see which way the wind is blowing—but first and foremost you'd want to set up a target and know just where it stood. After all, you can't hit a target if you don't have one, or if you're not sure where it's hidden.

Here's another saying: If you aim at nothing, you'll hit it every time! Before you can begin writing a speech, or even outlining one, you need to know your goal. If you used the exercise at the end of Lesson 5, you have already set up your target. Perhaps you're giving a persuasive speech, and you're intending to persuade your audience that the government should not set speed limits on the highway. The exercise in Lesson 5 helped you to enumerate the various points intended to prove that speed limits are bad, and it even had you list certain illustrations that will demonstrate each point.

If you skipped the exercise in the last lesson, go back and do it now! It will provide you with the bare bones you'll need to create this skeleton, and without bones and a skeleton, you'll find it difficult to bring your speech to life.

Speech Body Parts

A speech follows the same pattern as a well-constructed college essay, containing an introduction, sub-points, and conclusion. Think of these as the major body parts for your skeleton: head, torso, and feet. The head is your introduction, letting the audience know who they're listening to just as a face identifies a person. The body is where the living organs are, and it's where you'll concentrate all your facts, figures, examples, and illustrations. Finally, the feet give it mobility, just as a good conclusion will help your audience take your thoughts away with them.

We'll discuss each of these body parts in subsequent lessons, but for now you'll want to keep in mind that your outline will address each area. If it's not in the outline, it won't end up in the speech.

Introduction

The introduction is aptly named, because that's exactly what it does: It introduces your topic to the audience. You wouldn't be comfortable if some stranger walked up to you and simply started trying to sell you a dishwasher; you'd want to know his name and credentials and why you should buy a dishwasher from him. Similarly, your audience wants to know what you intend to tell them, what your topic is, what your goal is—and perhaps even who *you* are. If they don't already know you, they'll want to know your name and why you're qualified to be speaking on that particular topic.

So your introduction will be an important time to gain both the attention and the respect of your audience. See Lesson 9 for more information on what to include.

Body

The body will encompass the majority of your speech. It is the place where you will expand upon your theme and develop your topic or your persuasive argument. It's where you'll bring out all your facts and statistics, use visual aids, prove that your opinion is correct, and so forth.

This is the part of your outline that will force you to recognize what you know and what you don't know, and it will show you where more research is needed. It will also be constructed from the research that you've already done, and we'll discuss in a moment how to utilize that preliminary work. See Lesson 7 for more information on the body of your speech.

Conclusion

Remember that the conclusion represents the feet of your speech—it is what gives the speech mobility, enabling your audience to take your thoughts home with them. To that end, you will want to summarize your major points, stating clearly how the parts of your speech worked together to achieve your goal. If you're giving a persuasive speech, for example, your conclusion will state how the evidence you've provided proves that your thesis is true.

The primary purpose of a conclusion, of course, is to conclude—to end your speech in a memorable way. But it also helps your audience to *draw* a conclusion, to take the abstract information you've provided and apply it to their own lives. In this sense, the conclusion is more than a summary of your main points; it's

a time to show your audience that what you've said has practical value. See Lesson 8 for more information on how to do this.

Using Your Research

The preliminary research you conducted in Lesson 4 will now start to pay off. But that payoff will only be as great as the notes you've taken! That's why we emphasized so strongly the importance of including anything that might be of interest to you later. If you did jot down where those facts and statistics were located, you can now go back and get the specifics.

But before you actually start writing an outline, it will be important to organize your notes. I like to use spiral-bound notebooks when taking notes, but many people prefer to use index cards. Whatever you use to take notes, you'll want to categorize them by source and by topic. Here is an example of my own note-taking system that is categorized for an outline:

How to Paint Realistic Miniature Figures	
John Smith (NY: Painters Guild Press, 2010)	
12 paint selection; primer	"Primer is important because it covers the basic material with paint. Later layers will not adhere properly to metal or plastic, but they _will_ adhere to paint—and primer is what paint likes!"
13–17 modeling materials	Ceramic materials hold paint better than metal or plastic. Question: what about a primer coat? Is that needed on ceramic?
22 brushwork	"A smooth brush stroke is vitally important in any painting project."
22–29 brushwork	Smith outlines a variety of brushing styles here.
36 paint selection	"Paint selection is the lifeblood of any painting project. Selecting the wrong paint for your project is like eating poison—bad paint can kill your favorite figure."
38–43 paint selection? chemical compounds	Smith lists the chemical compositions of various paints; might be useful if I address technical issues

Notice that the very first thing I do when taking notes is to write down all the necessary citation information for that book or periodical at the top of the page. This is vitally important so that I can find the information again at a later date.

I then take notes in the main body of each page. Some notes are direct quotations, indicated by my use of quotation marks. When writing down a direct quotation, make certain that you have it written *exactly* as it is written in the original. Notice, for example, that I've underlined the word *will* in the first quotation. That indicates that the word was italicized in the book. If I were to use this quotation in a printed essay, I'd need to italicize that word just as it was in the original.

In the left-hand column, I write down the page number where I found that quotation or information. If there is a bulk of information that does not seem immediately pertinent, I summarize it with a short note and include the range of pages where it's found.

You can use this same approach to your note-taking, making it very easy to track something down later on. Of course, you'll have more than one page of notes. Every time you find information from a new source, you'll start a new page in your notebook, listing the exact citation at the top and specific page numbers in the margin.

Outlining from Your Notes

Suppose that you were preparing a how-to speech on the topic of painting miniature figures. It's your favorite hobby, so you already know a good deal about how it's done. You've also read several books and magazine articles on the topic and taken notes as you've gone along.

Now it's time to categorize those notes. Notice in my example that I've categorized each note as "paint selection," "brush work," and so forth, written beneath the page numbers in the left margin. This step is done when you're ready to start an outline, not during the actual research process—unless you know in advance

exactly what you'll be discussing in your speech. Most of the time, however, you'll find it most valuable to finish all your research before trying to categorize the information.

The categories are very important for two reasons: They enable you to decide what points you want to discuss in your speech, and they make it easy to find information on each point as you begin your outline.

So you read through your notes and decide that you want to talk specifically about various ways to use a paintbrush, different uses for different types of paint, and how to paint various types of material that a miniature figure is made from. Here is what your initial outline will look like:

I. Introduction
   A. TBD
II. Ways to use a paintbrush
   A. smooth strokes are best (Smith 22)
   B. but sometimes rough strokes add texture (Jones 43)
   C. [need more info on various strokes from Smith]
III. How to select paint
   A. "lifeblood" quote from Smith 36
   B. importance of primer (Smith 12; Jones 29; Brown 44)
   C. why paints are different—summarize Smith 38–43
IV. Different modeling materials
   A. metal (Jones 128–132)
   B. plastic (Brown 33–40)
   C. ceramic (Smith 13–17)
V. Conclusion
   A. TBD

You will notice several things from this initial outline. First, it is pretty sparse! This is an important feature of outlining: You are not actually writing the speech, you're just organizing your thoughts. So for now all you need is a short statement that will direct your thinking and writing in the next phase of the writing process. Remember that an outline is just a skeleton; you'll add flesh and muscle when you actually start writing.

You will also notice that the outline draws together your research information from all the sources you've consulted and organizes the information into a logical structure. This is where the categorization of your notes becomes so helpful, because you can scan through many pages of notes looking specifically for information on a particular point, ignoring all the rest that does not apply.

Finally, you'll notice that there is some information missing. When you were doing your research, you didn't think that Smith's information on various brush strokes would be pertinent to your speech—but now you think differently. Aren't you overjoyed that you wrote down where to find that information? Now you can quickly return to Smith's book and find the specifics you need to fill out that portion of your outline.

Conclusion

You might note that this lesson is constructed using the very pattern that we're discussing. It begins with an introduction, then goes into detail in the body, and here we are at the conclusion!

The main points you need to remember from this lesson are these: You *must* have an outline before you begin writing, or you won't know where you're going and how you'll get there; your outline will only be as good as your research notes, so learn to take notes efficiently; the outline is just a skeleton, providing short directions that you'll use when actually writing the speech.

Now it's time for you to put these theories into practice.

Exercise

Use this basic structure as a starting point to create an outline from your research notes:

I. Introduction
   A. Who am I? Why am I speaking?
   B. What will I speak about?
   C. What will the audience learn or gain from my presentation? Or what opinion do I intend to prove?

II. Point 1: The first step, piece of evidence, or important fact
   A. Details on this point
   B. Examples of this point
   C. Why this point is important to the overall topic

III. Point 2: The second step, piece of evidence, or important fact
   A. Details on this point
   B. Examples of this point
   C. Why this point is important to the overall topic

IV. Point 3: The third step, piece of evidence, or important fact
   A. Details on this point
   B. Examples of this point
   C. Why this point is important to the overall topic

V. Conclusion
   A. Summarize the main points
   B. Summarize how the points taught the skill, proved the thesis, or demonstrated the facts
   C. Draw a conclusion that is applicable to your audience

TIPS

- Your outline is just a skeleton, showing you the basic structure of your speech. You'll add flesh and muscle in the actual writing process.

- Your outline is only as good as your notes. Take good notes, and you'll write a good outline.

- Remember this rule when taking notes: When in doubt, *don't* leave it out!

- Be careful to include full citation information, including page numbers, when taking notes, so that you can find information later.

- If you aim at nothing, you'll hit it every time!

PREPARING AN OUTLINE

7 ▶ BODY BUILDING

Speech is the mirror of the soul; as a man speaks, so is he.

—Publilius Syrus, First Century b.c.

LESSON SUMMARY

The body of your speech contains the living organs, or the facts and information that define what you have to say. In this lesson, you will learn how to build that body.

Now that we have constructed a skeleton for our speech, we are ready to add some muscle and flesh to the bones. This is where the majority of the writing work takes place, so it makes the most sense to start here.

You may not be delivering your speech by reading from a fully written text; in fact, most of the time you won't want to. (We'll discuss this further in Lesson 10.) Nevertheless, it will be a very helpful exercise to write out your first speech word-for-word, exactly as you will deliver it. This will help you to understand a number of fundamental principles involved in good speech writing. In this lesson, we will address the most important part of your speech: the body.

As we discussed in Lesson 5, there are many types of speeches that you might find yourself asked to give, but all of them follow more or less the same pattern when constructing the body. Therefore, we will tackle the most challenging form of speech, the persuasive type, and use that as our template on how to create a powerful body. All other types of speeches will follow this pattern to some extent, even though the goal will not be to persuade the audience of an opinion. So if you are giving an informative speech or a demonstrative speech, you won't be concerned with the aspect of proving your opinion to be true, but you will still be able to use this structure to build the body of your speech.

Selecting Your Main Points

The first step in writing the body of your speech is to decide what your major points will be. You will tell the audience what your topic or thesis is in the introduction (which we'll cover in Lesson 9), so in the body you will want to start breaking down your topic into several major sub-points or aspects of that topic.

In the case of a persuasive speech, your subpoints will be the pieces of evidence you want to bring in to prove that your thesis—the opinion you stated in the introduction—is true. Before we go any further, however, we should briefly consider how many subpoints your speech should include. This will depend largely upon how much time you have to speak. If you have 20 minutes, you can probably include three subpoints; 10 minutes might restrict you to two; 40 minutes might permit four.

The main rule of thumb would be to have between two and five sub-points. Only one sub-point is not a sub-point at all; it's a secondary topic or thesis. More than five sub-points, on the other hand, becomes too much information. Remember our shotgun/rifle analogy: It's better to cover a few points in depth than a lot of points superficially.

Adding Flesh

You already created a preliminary outline in the last lesson, so let's use that to begin building a full speech. We'll use the outline that we created on the topic of painting miniatures as our example, even though it's not a persuasive speech. Here is the body portion of that outline:

II. Ways to use a paintbrush
   A. smooth strokes are best (Smith 22)
   B. but sometimes rough strokes add texture (Jones 43)
   C. [need more info on various strokes from Smith]

III. How to select paint
   A. "lifeblood" quote from Smith 36
   B. importance of primer (Smith 12; Jones 29; Brown 44)
   C. why paints are different—summarize Smith 38–43

IV. Different modeling materials
   A. metal (Jones 128–132)
   B. plastic (Brown 33–40)
   C. ceramic (Smith 13–17)

This is going to be a demonstrative speech, so you won't need to prove anything; rather, you'll need to *demonstrate* each of your sub-points in some manner, explaining to your audience how each sub-point is an important aspect of painting miniatures. This will be done both physically and verbally: You'll want to have visual aids that will illustrate your points and enable you to show your audience what you're talking about, but you'll also need to explain in clear language what you're doing and why you're doing it.

As you sit down to write, however, you might suddenly realize that your points are out of sensible order. You think through what you'll need to say for each point, and realize that it makes more sense to begin your speech with point 2 instead of point 1. So, your first point will now be "how to select paint." This will allow you to use a nice quotation from the Smith book early in your lecture, helping your audience to understand one of the most important elements of painting. You will want to put that into plain English in your speech, so you might write something like this:

> *One of the first important things to consider when painting miniatures is what paint you will use. As John Smith writes in his excellent book* How to Paint Realistic Miniature Figures, *"Paint selection is the lifeblood of any painting project. Selecting the wrong paint for your project is like eating poison—bad paint can kill your favorite figure." Therefore, the first step in painting miniatures is to choose an appropriate paint.*
>
> *There are, of course, many types and brands to choose from. As you can see [gesture to row of paints], it can be a bit intimidating to choose if you don't know what to look for. The best place to start is to select an appropriate primer to use as a base-coat on your figure, because a good primer will allow you to use some paints that might not adhere to your figure otherwise.*

I have taken the raw material from my outline and fleshed it out into a workable first draft of my speech. I introduce my first sub-point by explaining that paint selection is an important aspect of painting miniatures, and this leads naturally into the quotation from the Smith book.

I next work in my first visual aid, which will be a row of paints set up in front of the podium. By gesturing to them, I am working them into my speech, giving the audience a nice visual aid to bring my words to life, while also not permitting them to become a distraction *from* my words.

Next, I move onto the importance of selecting a primer, following my outline, and will spend a paragraph or two in the speech explaining how to

do so. But notice one other thing that I did in that last sentence: I explained *why* primer selection is important to my topic.

Explaining the Significance of Your Sub-Points

This is the step in speech writing that many beginners omit, but it's one of the most important elements in a successful speech. It is not good enough to tell your audience that something is important or that something is true; you must also tell them *why* it's important or true.

Let's return to the example that we used in Lesson 5, where you are a lawyer in a court trying to prove that John Smith murdered Bill Jones. Your introduction will contain your thesis, that John Smith shot Bill Jones, so the body of your speech will consist of presenting several points of evidence and explaining how each piece of evidence proves your thesis. Here again is the outline we used for that example:

Thesis: John Smith murdered Bill Jones.

Evidence 1: Here is the revolver that he used to shoot him.

Explanation: It has been proven that this gun fired the fatal bullet, and Smith's fingerprints were found on the handle.

Evidence 2: Jones and Smith were seen arguing just before the shooting.

Explanation: Smith was angry with Jones and threatened to kill him, and three witnesses heard him just prior to the gunshots.

Evidence 3: Smith has no alibi for where he was at the time of the shooting.

Explanation: Since Smith was seen by witnesses at the scene just moments before the crime, it is beyond doubt that he committed it.

Conclusion: There is no reasonable doubt that John Smith shot Bill Jones.

If this court case were constructed as a speech, each piece of evidence would consist of a major sub-point in your presentation. Point 1 would be to show your audience a revolver and tell them that it was the gun used to kill the victim. But showing them the gun is not enough to prove that John Smith is guilty—you must also explain how that gun proves his guilt.

Imagine a lawyer standing up in court and showing a gun to the jury. He says, "See this gun? It was used to shoot Bill Jones! So now you know that John Smith is guilty." Then he sits down.

Has that lawyer proven his case? Obviously not. Now ask yourself what was missing from his presentation, and you'll immediately recognize that he needed to explain how that gun was connected to John Smith as well as to the murder. No matter how convincing the lawyer's evidence might have been, it was worthless without a clear explanation of how it proved his thesis.

This principle is equally true of your speech. It won't matter how well prepared you are, how much research you've done, or how much of an expert you are on your topic; if you don't explain to your audience how each sub-point supports your thesis, your speech will miss its goal.

Fortunately, however, we already thought about that detail and included it in our outline. The gun proves Smith's guilt because his fingerprints were found on the handle. Similarly, the selection of a correct primer is important in painting miniatures because it allows the painter to use a wider variety of paints. In both these examples, the speaker has given the audience a clear understanding of how the sub-point relates to the thesis. The goal of the persuasive speech will be furthered because the audience will understand how one piece of evidence proves the truth of the speaker's opinion; the goal of the demonstrative speech is furthered because the audience understands how primer selection relates to their own hobby of painting.

Arranging Your Sub-Points

When we sat down to write our speech on miniature painting, we decided to rearrange our sub-points, moving point 2 up to point 1. The reason for this was simply that it made more logical sense to begin with that point, since the other two points built upon the selection of paint. In other words, to begin with the foundational point and build upon it with subsequent points made for a more logical flow of thought.

This is one of the most commonly used methods to determine how to arrange the sub-points in one's speech. Here are some other methods you can use:

- **Topical:** If your main topic is broken down into sub-topics, then arrange those points by topic. An example of this might be the main point "How to Plan an Ideal Vacation." Sub-topics of this might include "Look for the Best Prices," "Choose a Suitable Climate," and "Travel at Off-Times."
- **Chronological:** You can arrange your points in chronological order, either forward in time or backward. You might be speaking about the history of your club, and you could begin at its origins and move through significant events up to the present. Or you might want to demonstrate where the present economic crisis originated, starting in the present and working your way back through recent history.
- **Cause and Effect:** This is a very useful method when creating a persuasive speech. Your points might be three or four current problems in the health-care industry, and at each point you would explain what caused that problem and what effect it has on health care. This method would focus on the root causes of issues, rather than on their solutions.

- **Problem and Solution:** This is a variation of the cause-and-effect method, in which you would focus instead on the solutions of the existing problems without being too concerned with where those problems originated. Your points would then be organized into three or four major problems about which your audience is concerned, offering solutions to each.
- **Step-by-Step:** This is similar to the chronological method in the sense that you will address one step that must be fulfilled before the next step can be started. It's useful in demonstrative speeches, such as the miniature painting example used earlier.

Writing and Rewriting

Finally, it is worth touching upon the question of writing styles at this point, although we will delve into this topic in greater depth as we go along. But at this point, you might be feeling somewhat overwhelmed at the prospect of taking that skeletal outline and converting it into a lively, interesting speech. Don't be dismayed—you are not alone!

For many, there is nothing quite so intimidating as a blank sheet of paper you must fill with words. I've been a writer in various fields for more than 30 years, and I still feel that sense of intimidation when I first sit down to begin a writing project. This is just as true when writing a speech as it is when writing a book, because both are dependent upon words and ideas. You might have the most brilliant ideas for your speech, but they won't be worth much if you can't put them into suitable words.

The most important thing to understand now is that you are beginning your *first draft*, not your completed speech. The words that you put on paper or type

into your computer are not the final words that you will speak before an audience; they are merely the beginning. Once you have gone through your outline, you will want to go back and make changes.

One of the most important areas of change will involve those gaps you discover as you write the first draft. You already discovered some gaps when you converted your raw notes into an outline; now you'll most likely discover a few more as you flesh out the skeleton. As I said previously, you never know how much you know until you try to explain it to someone else. Putting your outline into fully written form will bring to light areas where your information is incomplete, or where you need better examples to illustrate your points.

This might involve some further research, or it might mean going back to one of your previous sources for more information. Whatever is required to fill those gaps, you will have to return to your first draft and make some changes to add the new information. You might also feel that your wording isn't as good as it could be in some portions, and this will require that you go back through your speech and do some rewriting.

Rewriting is the hardest concept for beginners to grasp, and many first-time public speakers simply skip the step. Those who do, however, rarely make that same mistake a second time—the embarrassment of delivering a poorly written speech is a strong deterrent. You must remember that you will be essentially reading what you've written in front of an audience, so you should make sure that it's written well in the first place.

It may seem like a lot of unnecessary work at this point, especially if you are planning to deliver your speech from an outline or from notes, rather than reading a fully written speech. We will discuss these various methods of speech delivery in a later lesson, but for now this exercise is very important because it helps you to think through exactly what you intend to say when you get up to speak.

It is an easy temptation to think that once you've put your outline together, you're ready to get up and speak. You're not! You need to know in advance what you're going to say—*exactly* what you're going to say— at each point in your speech. The best way to do this when you're first learning how to speak publicly is to write out your speech verbatim, and then read it aloud to yourself. This will show you the areas of weakness and help you discover ways to improve.

So take the time and effort to do some rewriting on your first draft. You will be immensely glad you did when you get up to speak.

Writing for Speaking, Not Reading

Remember that you are writing a speech, not a novel. This distinction influences the length of your speech as well as the style. And the best way to understand both those distinctions is to read your speech out loud once it's written, pretending that you are actually delivering it in front of the audience.

You will be quick to notice areas where your wording is uncomfortable or unnatural to you as you speak them aloud. The words might read well, but a speech is meant to be heard, not read. This exercise will help you to understand that distinction, and will help you to cultivate your own natural speaking style.

Reading your speech aloud will also help you to smooth transitions between points. In our figure-painting speech, the three main points are not closely related at first glance, so we'll want to make some sort of transition when moving from point 1 to point 2. It's easy to forget this when you're writing, but speaking it out loud as though you were in front of an audience will make you recognize when transitions are rough.

Finally, time yourself as you read through the first draft to see how long it takes to deliver the speech. Most people have a great fear of not having enough to say when they give a speech, and the most common solution is to include far more information than you think you'll need. That's not a bad approach in your first draft, since it's easier to cut information than to add it. All the same, don't be afraid to make those cuts if your speech takes too long. Conversely, if you've been asked to speak for 15 minutes and your speech only takes three, you'll need to bolster it with more information, better examples, some anecdotes, and so forth. It's true that you have not yet written the introduction and conclusion, but those elements add only a small portion of time to the overall speech. Plus, reading aloud through just the body will frequently make the introduction and conclusion practically write themselves.

Exercise
Use this questionnaire after reading aloud through the first draft of your body:

- How long did the body of my speech take to read aloud? What is my target time window?
- If it's too long, what needs to be cut? If it's too short, what needs to be added?
- What weaknesses did I find? (missing information, poor illustrations, weak explanations, etc.)
- How can I strengthen those areas? Where will I find the information to do so?
- Did I successfully persuade (or inform or teach) my audience? If not, how did I fail?
- Do I have enough main points? Too many?
- Are my main points well organized?
- Do I have smooth transitions from one point to the next?
- What further research do I need?

TIPS

- Remember to explain each of your major points, telling the audience why that point is relevant to your topic and how it applies to them.

- As a general rule, your speech should have no fewer than three major points and no more than five.

- A speech is written to be heard, not read.

- Some ways to organize your points include:

  Topical

  Chronological

  Cause and Effect

  Problem and Solution

  Step-by-Step

8 ▶ END WITH A BANG

To succeed, jump as quickly at opportunities as you do at conclusions.
—BENJAMIN FRANKLIN, 1706–1790

LESSON SUMMARY
What you say in your conclusion will become the most memorable part of your speech to the audience, so make it short and make it good!

Now that you have the body of your speech in good working order, you are ready to write the conclusion. When you created your outline, you made a sort of road map that enabled you to know where you were going and how you would get there. Now that you've finished detailing the route on your speech journey, you are ready to tell your audience where you arrived and how you got there.

Many speakers, however, tend to treat their conclusions as if they were self-evident. After all, they reason, I've spent 30 minutes explaining my topic—surely they get it by now! But the sad fact is that the audience might *not* get it, even after you've covered your topic in depth. They might understand all the points you've made and enjoyed your illustrations and examples, but they might not have stopped to consider what your topic means to them personally.

This is the "punch" of a good conclusion: It enables your audience to summarize your major points and apply them to their own experience. The body of your speech might have shown the audience how to paint miniature figures, but it's the conclusion that will help them understand how that knowledge applies to their own hobby. You might have outlined many good reasons to prefer toothpaste A over B, but it will be the conclusion that urges the audience to switch brands.

The conclusion is the compressed information that the audience will take home with them. If you're a computer user, you are probably familiar with .zip files, which contain compressed documents. The .zip file takes many large documents and squeezes them into their smallest size, gathers them all together, and encapsulates them into one small file. That is the role of the conclusion: It takes many large points, compresses them into several small snippets, explains how to use them, and sends them home with the audience.

The conclusion of your speech is aptly named, because it does two things: It *concludes* the speech, bringing it to a close; and it *draws conclusions* about your topic. To do this, a good conclusion will be brief, and it will:

- Restate your original thesis
- Summarize your major points
- Provide closure
- Call the audience to action

Restate Your Thesis

If you are giving a persuasive speech, your thesis will be the opinion you intend to prove. The thesis of an informative or demonstrative speech will be the knowledge or skill you intend to impart to your audience. As you open your conclusion, you will want to remind your audience of the reason why you were speaking to them in the first place.

The reason that this is important is not that the audience is unintelligent. No public speaker should ever fall prey to that line of thinking! The reason for reiterating your thesis is that it gets the audience to take a step back from focusing on the details of your speech and helps them to start looking at the big picture.

Summarize Your Major Points

You divided the body of your speech into several major points, and you went into each point in detail. Those points are critical to the success of your speech—they are the evidence that proves your thesis, the highways that you used to reach your destination, and the flesh and muscle that brought your skeleton to life!

It is important, therefore, to reiterate those points so that the audience can see the big picture of how they got to that destination. The important thing to understand, however, is that you are merely encapsulating those points—you are *not* repeating them in detail. Just a few words on each point will suffice.

Provide Closure

The closing of your speech accomplishes two important things: It summarizes the big picture of where you arrived and how you got there, and it lets the audience know that the speech has concluded. Remember what we said earlier: A conclusion both *concludes* and *draws conclusions*.

You let your audience know that your speech is ending—but only when it really is! Nothing will frustrate your listeners more than hearing you say, "In conclusion. . . ," only to have you drone on for another ten minutes. Remember that your audience will begin to think about other things when your speech ends, so you don't want to lose their attention before you're done.

Helping them to draw conclusions about your topic is important, because it finishes the larger picture you've been trying to paint in their minds. It reminds them that the things you've been discussing have some implications for their own lives, and this reminder leads you naturally into the last aspect of your conclusion.

Call the Audience to Action

Neither you nor the audience have gathered together just to kill time. You have all come to the lecture in order to learn something—and knowledge without practical application is useless. Your conclusion, therefore, should tell the audience how your speech applies to their own lives.

A demonstrative speech is useful to your audience only if they take that skill and start using it themselves. A persuasive speech has not fully convinced the audience until they deliberately act upon their newly acquired opinion. An informative speech that spews out facts and figures is of no value if the audience doesn't know how to *use* that information.

You have chosen to speak on a topic about which you're very knowledgeable, so ask yourself these questions: Why have I become knowledgeable about this topic? How do I use this knowledge in my daily life? What has been the value of this knowledge to me? When you figure out these answers, you have the information for your conclusion.

Be Brief

Finally, remember that your conclusion is a summary; it is not an exposition. You have expounded upon your topic in depth in the body of your speech; you are merely reiterating those points at the end.

Do not try to introduce new information into your conclusion. If you think of something that you omitted while writing your conclusion, go back to the body and add it in there—or omit it altogether. Remember that your audience may stop listening when they sense that the speech is almost over, and any new information will be wasted. Think of your own classroom experiences: When the bell rang in high school, the students stopped listening to the teacher. The same thing will happen when you conclude your speech.

Concluding Our Examples

Let's return to the speech examples that we used earlier—the comparison of toothpastes A and B, and the skill of painting miniature figures. Here are examples of how we might conclude each of those speeches:

Toothpaste Speech:

As you can see, ladies and gentlemen, all toothpastes are not created equal! Toothpaste A is not the same as toothpaste B in the matter of effectiveness, for we have clearly demonstrated that A fights cavities far beyond the capabilities of B. The two brands are not on equal footing when it comes to personal appearance, either—after all, who wants green teeth when a bright smile is so readily available in a tube of toothpaste A? And the two brands are certainly not equal in price—and in this area alone, toothpaste B far surpasses A, costing nearly twice as much at any local pharmacy. In these ways, we can clearly see that toothpaste A is better than toothpaste B.

What remains is entirely up to you. Will you continue to use an inferior product that costs more? Or will you see the light of good sense and switch to toothpaste A? The choice is clear: Buy toothpaste A!

Painting Speech:

We have covered a number of important aspects of miniature painting today, all of which will help you to improve your techniques and get more pleasure from painting. The major things to remember before starting your next project are these: Select the right paint for the job, use your paintbrush to its maximum capabilities, and understand the demands and drawbacks of the figure's basic material.

When you keep these important elements in mind, you will decrease the frustrations and increase the rewards of this captivating hobby. But remember this above all else: You can't learn a skill unless you practice, and the best time to practice is today! Take these tips home with you and get started right away—you'll be glad you did.

Exercise

Use this questionnaire together with the body of your speech to outline your conclusion:

- **Thesis:** What did I hope to prove? What goal was I aiming at?

- **Main points:** What pieces of evidence did I use, or what steps did I take to reach my conclusion? (Summarize the points in one sentence each.)
- **Closure:** What did I accomplish in this speech? What conclusion can I draw? What skill have I taught, or what opinion have I proven?
- **Action:** What practical application does this information offer? How do I use it in my own life? Why will it matter to my audience?

TIPS

- Be brief. Your audience may stop listening when they sense the end approaching.

- Do not introduce new information in the conclusion.

- The conclusion *concludes* and it *draws conclusions*.

- Knowledge without practical application is useless. Tell the audience how to *use* the information you've provided.

END WITH A BANG

9 ▶ START WITH A BANG

To persuade a man, you must first gain his attention.

—ANCIENT PROVERB

LESSON SUMMARY

An introduction simply introduces: It introduces something new, or it introduces some new element of something already known. Learn how to get and hold the audience's attention by creating a strong introduction.

You might be wondering why you're writing your introduction last, rather than first. After all, the introduction is the opening of your speech, so wouldn't it make more sense to begin at the beginning?

The introduction of your speech tells your audience where you'll be going and how you'll get there—but you can't really be sure of those details until you have actually written the speech! For example, the introduction to this book was the very last thing I wrote, even though I worked from an outline. Books and speeches in some measure write themselves, and you cannot be entirely sure of what your final product will be until it's finished.

Therefore, it makes more sense to write your introduction after you know clearly what it is that you'll be introducing. And now that you've written the bulk of your speech, you're ready to do that.

To summarize the role of your introduction: "Tell them what you're going to tell them; tell them; then tell them what you told them." In fact, the introduction is similar to the conclusion in many ways. You'll state your thesis, outline the major points, and explain how your topic will be of value to the audience. The only thing missing is a call to action, and even that has a counterpart when you give them a reason to listen. Here are the major things to accomplish in your introduction:

- Keep the audience's attention
- State your credentials
- Introduce your topic or thesis
- Introduce your major sub-points
- Give them a reason to listen

Keep the Audience's Attention

When you first walk to the front to give your speech, you will have the audience's attention—so your job is to keep it! Understand, however, that they may be paying attention for all the wrong reasons. They might wonder who that stranger is, or they might wonder why *you* were selected to speak instead of them. They might be evaluating your taste in fashion, checking your ring finger to see if you're married, comparing you to the previous speaker, or admiring your new haircut. And a few might even be wondering what interesting things you're going to say.

Whatever their reason for paying attention, you don't want to waste that moment. The trick is to get the audience to stop paying attention to *you* and start paying attention to *your words*. Actually, the first part of that equation is fairly simple; the fact is, the moment you start to speak, most of the audience will lose interest in whatever had their attention a moment before. Your job is to transfer that attention to your words and not let it wander away.

Here are some techniques you can use to accomplish that task:

- **Use a quotation.** You've probably noticed that each chapter in this book starts with a quotation. Notice that each is short, capturing the essence of the lesson in a few words. Many are

also humorous. These are good guidelines in finding suitable quotations.

- **Tell an anecdote or joke.** Like the quotation, however, make it short and to the point. It should lead naturally into the topic that you'll be speaking about.
- **Cite a startling fact.** It can be a real attention-getter to start with something like this: "We all use toothpaste, but did you know that potassium cyanide is the main ingredient in some brands?" Just make sure that your facts are correct.
- **Cite a historic event.** This is particularly useful on special occasions. "Just ten years ago today, this lovely couple first met at the National Pie-Eating finals."
- **Cite a current event.** This is a very useful way to introduce a persuasive speech. "In light of the recent events in Washington, it is our duty to consider ways to reform our judicial system."

State Your Credentials

It is possible that you will be speaking to an organization of which you are a member, and the audience may already know you quite well. It is even possible that the common bond that draws you all together is the very topic that you'll be speaking about, such as you'd have with a photography club or musicians' organization. Yet even then, they may not know about your extensive knowledge on some branch of that common bond, and they won't know how your topic has enriched your life. And the fact is that most of your experiences speaking in public will *not* be to such an audience; you may often be addressing a group of people who know very little about you.

Whether or not your audience knows you personally, you will want to acquaint them with your credentials. They will wonder why you are qualified to teach them about your topic; they will want to know how *you* know what you're talking about. Put yourself in your listener's place: You would not be likely to change your brand of toothpaste just because some stranger accosts you on the street and starts rattling off facts and figures. You would be far more likely to accept the recommendation of a bona fide dentist, because this person has the credentials to know what he or she is talking about.

You are not going to give the audience your autobiography here; you will want to focus specifically on things that give you credibility regarding your speech topic—and nothing more.

Here are a few things that can boost your credibility:

- **Dress appropriately.** Anticipate how your audience will dress—then go one notch better. If they'll be in jeans and t-shirts, then you should wear dress slacks and an oxford shirt, and so forth.
- **Be prepared.** Nothing builds your confidence as well as knowing what you're about to say.
- **Stand up straight.** It's a common temptation to slouch when nervous, so be conscious of this as you walk to the front. Stand straight with your chin up and look directly out at the audience as you begin to speak.
- **Know your credentials—and theirs.** Telling an audience of rocket scientists about your experiences with paper airplanes won't gain you credibility. Know in advance where your strengths lie and then tell them to the audience.

Introduce Your Topic or Thesis

The purpose of an introduction is to introduce. That may sound self-evident, but think about its implications. You can be introduced to something or someone that you've never encountered before; and you can have something that is very familiar introduced to your attention; you can even be introduced to a whole new aspect of someone or something that you have long thought you understood fully.

This is just how an introduction works. It introduces the topic to the audience, whether they are deeply knowledgeable on it or not. It focuses on what the audience already knows, and tells them how you're going to show them something they *don't* know. Fortunately, you covered this base in Lesson 1 when you analyzed the audience. By this point, you know what topics are of interest to your listeners, and you also know how deep their knowledge is on your topic.

Remember this important fact: If the audience thinks they already know what you're going to say, they won't listen; if they think you've got some new information, they will. Your introduction must cater to this "need to know."

Introduce Your Major Sub-Points

This will be a natural extension of the introduction of your topic or thesis. If you tell the audience that you're going to prove some startling opinion, you will also want to tell them what main pieces of proof you'll be offering. If you are addressing a topic with which the audience is already familiar, then you'll be stressing the aspects of your speech that will be new to them.

Remember the adage we opened with: "Tell them what you'll tell them; tell them; then tell them what you told them." You are only telling them what points you're going to cover; you're not actually covering them yet—so keep it brief. Introduce each point with one sentence at the most.

Give Them a Reason to Listen

This is essentially the same technique that you used in your conclusion when you provided closure—except that this time you're providing an opener. This is the big picture that we mentioned in the last lesson, or the overview of where you're going and *why* you're going there. This is the time to tell the audience how your speech will influence their lives.

You don't need to get into specifics here; you'll do that in the conclusion. All the same, the audience will be interested in listening if they know that your talk will have real-life, practical application in their lives. This is the time to let them know how your speech will be useful to them.

Be Brief

Like the conclusion, your introduction is merely a summary; it is not the body of the speech. If you have crafted it well, your audience will actually be eager to hear what you have to say—so get going!

Introducing Our Examples

Let's return once again to our speech examples. Here are ways that we might introduce each of those speeches:

Toothpaste Speech:

Good morning, and thank you for coming today. And believe me in this: You'll be glad you did, because today I'm going to change your life. In fact, I'm going to change your very smile—I'm going to offer you a better reason to smile!

Nice smiles are a passion of mine. When I was six years old, I managed to knock most of my teeth out by riding my bicycle into a tree. That experience taught me two things: Trees are hard, and teeth are important. Fortunately, my adult teeth came in to replace them, but I've spent most of my life learning how to take proper care of that set—because they can't be replaced!

And that is just what we'll be discussing here this morning: how to protect your smile. I'm sure you all use toothpaste every day, but are you sure

you're using the best toothpaste? I'd like to offer you a comparison which will demonstrate that all toothpastes are not created alike; in fact, some are remarkably better than others. To that end, we'll consider three important elements of toothpaste selection: cavity prevention, whitening effects, and cost. When we're done, I think you'll agree that toothpaste A outperforms all its competitors, namely toothpaste B—and this is what is going to change your life.

First, let's consider the element of cavity protection. . . .

Painting Speech:

Good afternoon, it's a real privilege to be invited to speak to such an illustrious group of artists! I've had the pleasure of seeing some of your own painting projects, and I was deeply impressed by the measure of expertise and artistry in them. I was awed by the lifelike qualities in several horses, and when I got to the section of military miniatures. . . well, I was ready to surrender!

I've been painting miniatures since I was old enough to smear my fingerprints on my mom's newly painted white walls, which was also around the time I learned not to eat the paint. My own specialty is in the realm of fantasy figures, since I have a real passion for anything that looks remotely medieval. I've brought a few of my own favorites, which I'll have here on the table for you to check out when we're done.

I'd like to consider some of the finer points of brushwork and paint selection this afternoon, paying particular attention to how the miniature's construction influences those decisions. We'll start with the various types of paint, discussing more than just the basics as we consider what works best in different conditions. Then we'll turn our attention to the actual brushwork techniques we can use to accomplish different effects, and we'll conclude by considering how different media can limit and expand our horizons. By the time we're done, I think you'll be armed to make intelligent decisions on how to paint before you paint—and this can only improve your final product.

Let's begin with the most important decision: which paint to use. . . .

Exercise

Use this questionnaire together with the body of your speech to outline your introduction:

- **Attention grabber:** How can I best keep the audience's attention? What would I *not* want to draw attention to?

- **Credentials:** What makes me an expert on this topic? What does the audience already know? What new information can I offer them?

- **Topic:** What will I prove in this speech? What aspects of my topic will I focus on?

- **Sub-Points:** What are my sub-points? How does each point further my thesis or topic?

- **Application:** Why should the audience care about listening? What is in it for them? What will they take home with them?

TIPS

- You have the audience's attention when you walk to the front. Your job is to keep it!

- You want the audience to pay attention to your words, not your appearance.

- Always dress one notch better than your audience. Consider these dress categories:

    —Casual: Jeans, tennis shoes, t-shirts

    —Business Casual: Khakis, slacks, casual shirts and blouses, loafers

    —Business Formal: Suits, dresses, dress shoes, neckties

    —Formal: Tuxedoes, formal gowns, matching accessories

- "Tell them what you're going to tell them; tell them; then tell them what you told them."

- Give them a reason to listen—or they won't.

10 ▶ DON'T LOSE YOUR PLACE

That speech is most worth listening to which has been carefully prepared in private and tried on a plaster cast, or an empty chair, or any other appreciative object that will keep quiet, until the speaker has got his matter and his delivery limbered up so that they will seem impromptu to an audience.

—Mark Twain, 1835–1910

LESSON SUMMARY

No good speech is truly given off the cuff without some advance thought—but the best ones appear that way. In this lesson, we will consider the four major methods of speech delivery, noting the best uses of each.

The most common source of anxiety for those speaking publicly is the fear that they will get up front and suddenly go blank, forgetting everything they had planned to say. This fear is probably as common as dreaming that you are out in public without your pants—and it has about the same likelihood of actually happening in real life.

All the same, you can vastly alleviate those anxieties by the simple expedient of being well-prepared, knowing that you will not forget your words because you have taken vigorous steps to prevent that from happening. The truth is that unless you are giving an impromptu speech, you will have spent vast amounts of time researching and preparing your speech. The next step, then, is to decide how you will deliver it.

There are four common methods for delivering a speech:

- Reading from a manuscript
- Memorization
- Extemporaneous
- Impromptu

Reading from a Manuscript

The best and surest way to guarantee that you won't forget your speech is to write it down, word for word, and then read it back to your audience. This will certainly alleviate your anxiety—but it will also make a dreadfully dull speech.

You may have endured a teacher or professor who reads his lectures verbatim. If so, you have no doubt heard students remark, "Why doesn't he just give us all a copy of his lectures and let us read them ourselves?" This is precisely the response that you can expect from your audience if you should choose to read a fully written speech.

Having said that, there are undeniably occasions where it is best to read a written speech. Politicians, for example, do this on a regular basis (or else they memorize them, which we'll discuss in a moment) because it ensures that their wording is carefully crafted to avoid saying the wrong thing, or saying the right thing the wrong way. If you find yourself forced to read a pre-written speech, follow these guidelines:

- **Practice it—repeatedly.** Read it aloud with a red pen in hand, and notice any area where the writing does not flow smoothly when spoken. Reword that passage immediately—out loud—until it seems like something you'd say naturally; then write down the new wording.
- **Do not stare fixedly at your manuscript.** Practice looking up frequently, making eye contact with your audience. Do this especially at the ends of sentences and paragraphs.
- **Do not speak in monotone.** Vary the pitch of your voice, just as you would in normal speech. This does take some practice to make it sound natural, but you're going to practice repeatedly anyway.
- **Use a marker or finger to keep your place.** When I've been forced to give a speech from a manuscript, I've used a six-inch ruler, which I slide down the page as I go along. This is very unobtrusive, and it underlines the entire sentence on the page. You could also use your finger to mark each successive line of text as you go.
- **Design the page for easy reading.** I do this when I speak from an outline (my usual method), and it's even more important when reading verbatim. Double-space your text, using a large font that is easy to read. Double-space between paragraphs (four spaces total) rather than indenting. Do not break pages mid-paragraph; force a page break at the beginning of a paragraph, even if the previous page comes up short.
- **Use normal gestures and movement.** This is where a manuscript can get tricky, because it naturally glues you to the podium. Yet motion and gestures are vitally important to keeping your audience's attention, as we'll discuss more fully in a later lesson, so you'll want to practice reading the manuscript as though you were speaking naturally. This includes hand gestures from time to time, which means that you could potentially lose your place if you're using a finger—which is another good reason for finding a suitable marker like a ruler.
- **Practice it—repeatedly.** Just in case you forgot this crucial step.

Memorizing a Pre-Written Speech

By the time you have rehearsed your written speech—repeatedly—you will have it nearly memorized. It's a small step to rehearse it a few times more, deliberately committing it to memory in its entirety.

This method is better than reading directly from your manuscript, although it's not the best approach. It still runs the risk of sounding mechanical and contrived, but there are some ways of avoiding that.

- **Have your written manuscript in front of you.** You don't really need it anymore, but you may still be nervous enough that you might forget the speech midstream. With the manuscript in front of you, you'll be able to glance down if that should happen. You can still keep pace with your delivery by turning pages as you go, even without more than an occasional glance at the page. And that is all you want—an occasional glance. Most of the time, you'll keep your head up and eyes on the audience.

- **Speak in a conversational tone.** This is essentially what we stated for reading the speech directly off the page, but it is easier to avoid speaking in monotone when you've memorized what it is you're going to say. Vary the pitch and pace of your voice, just as you would when speaking naturally. The danger of memorized speeches is that the delivery can sound robotic. You've probably said the Pledge of Allegiance in groups before; just think how people sound when they say it: "*I pledge allegiance . . . to the flag . . . of the United States . . . of America . . . .*" Now try saying those same words out loud, as though you were speaking to a friend, and you'll realize that those odd pauses are very unnatural. A more natural delivery of the Pledge would sound something

like this: "I pledge *allegiance* to the flag of the *United States* of *America, and* to the Republic for which it stands—one nation under God—indivisible! With liberty and justice for all." The italicized words represent places where you would naturally add a verbal emphasis, and you'll note that the pauses are slight and in more appropriate locations. As you practice memorizing your speech, pay attention to how you sound, and strive to make your voice flow naturally.

- **Memorize your outline as well as your speech.** This is extra work, it's true, but it will pay huge dividends. It will enable you to visualize exactly where you are in your speech at all times, and you'll know which point follows your present point in case the exact wording should suddenly escape you.

- **Remember that nobody but you will know if you don't quote exactly.** In the dire event that you should suddenly go blank and not have the manuscript in front of you, just improvise on the spot. You memorized the outline, so you know roughly where you are and where you're going next. Just start talking about that next point. The exact wording will most likely come back to mind as you move forward—plus, by improvising, you've started experimenting with a highly effective method of speech delivery.

Speaking Extemporaneously

When you forgot the exact wording of your memorized speech and started to improvise, you were speaking extemporaneously. This is just a big word meaning that you come up with the exact wording as you go along. (The Latin word literally means "out of time," which is often the situation that forces a speaker to think up the delivery on the spot—since time has run out.)

An extemporaneous speech is not invented on the spot, however. It is actually thought out well in advance, and all the steps we've taken thus far in crafting a speech are used to prepare an extemporaneous speech—except the step of writing it out word for word. Instead, the extemporaneous speech is delivered from an outline or from rough notes, which are often printed on index cards.

This outline is not the one you created in Lesson 6, however. That was just a preliminary outline to get you started. This is the step you took in Lessons 7 through 9, where you wrote out the body, conclusion, and introduction verbatim. In the case of an extemporaneous speech, you would still take those steps, except that you won't write them verbatim; you'll make an outline or rough notes on what you'll say at those points and go from there.

Here is an outline I would use if I were giving the speech on painting miniatures:

I.   Greeting
     A. Thanks for invite
     B. Mention some of their projects [**examine in advance, fill in below**]
         1.
         2.
         3.
     C. Credentials:
         1. been painting since I was six years old
         2. fantasy figures
     D. Topic: brushwork and paint, figure materials
         1. types of paint
         2. brushwork
         3. media
II. Types of paint
     A. John Smith, *How to Paint Realistic Miniature Figures*
         1. "Paint selection is the lifeblood of any painting project. Selecting the wrong paint for your project is like eating poison—bad paint can kill your favorite figure."
     B. Many to choose from
         1. [**set up paint samples in front of room**]
     C. Primer = best starting point
         1. important for base coat
         2. allows variety of paints to adhere that might not otherwise
     D. Why paints are different

You'll notice several things about this outline. First, it's brief. It does not provide the exact wording you'll use when speaking; it only gives you the information you need to remember what you intend to say at each point. This enables you to keep your eyes on your audience more than on your notes, while it also prevents you from getting lost.

You'll also notice that I've included bracketed lines. I deliberately boldface such instructions in my own outlines so that I can see them easily in advance, enabling me to do my preliminary work before I get up front to speak. So this technique would remind you to examine the figures painted by your audience and to set up some paints to use as a visual aid beforehand.

I leave a few blank lines in my outline to fill in just before speaking. I do this because I intend to examine the painted miniatures that the audience brings with them, but I don't know what they'll be until I get there. Once I've seen them, I jot down a few brief notes in my outline just prior to speaking, and then mention the specifics in my introduction.

Notice also that the entire Smith quotation is written out in full. When quoting someone, you *don't* rely on extemporaneous invention because you need to get the words exactly correct. At this one point, you would be reading directly from your speech. Yet it also enables you to glance ahead to your next point so that you can then return your eyes to the audience.

Clearly, the extemporaneous speech is often the most effective method because it sounds spontaneous even though it is well rehearsed. People enjoy listening to someone who speaks conversationally rather than to someone rehashing a canned lecture, and this method achieves that end. Here are some tips to remember:

- **Practice!** This may come as a surprise, given that you haven't written out the text and you're not memorizing anything—yet that means it's even more important to practice. You will be more confident if you know approximately what you will say at each point on your outline, even though you are not trying to memorize exact wording.

- **Make changes to your outline.** Another benefit of practice is you will think of things to say that are not in your outline, and you may discover things that *are* in your outline that don't work. Mark the outline as you go, and then make those changes to your computer file.

- **Use a computer.** This is probably self-evident to most in our present computer age, but just in case: A computer document is easy to change and adjust handwritten pages are not. Computers also allow you to use a clear, easy-to-read font.

- **Use a clear, easy-to-read font.** In case it wasn't clear in the previous point, legibility is as important in your outline as it would be in a written speech. I use a decent-sized font with double-spacing for ease of reading.

- **Do not write out a lot of text—but make sure it's enough.** Your outline notes are intended to jog your memory on what you want to say next, but they're only a memory-jogger, not a puppet master. You want those notes to be clearly meaningful to you at the time of delivery, without being so wordy that you begin to read verbatim. Find a balance that works for you.

- **Practice some more.** Every time you make an adjustment to your outline, you should rehearse the entire speech again. Yes, it's a lot of work, but it makes the difference between mediocrity and excellence. Strive for excellence.

Impromptu Speeches

We touched on this type of speech earlier when we considered special occasion speeches, noting that they can be the most intimidating type of speech. But the fact is that you give impromptu speeches all the time—you just don't realize it. When you get together with a group of friends to hang out and talk, you are making an impromptu speech. When a professor asks you a question in class, you answer with an impromptu speech.

An impromptu speech is one that is given on the spur of the moment, without advance notice. Ironically, the Latin phrase *in promptu* (from which this word is drawn) actually means "to have at hand, to be in readiness." And this little piece of etymology gives away the big secret: The best impromptu speeches are not really unprepared at all, they are just given promptly!

You'll remember that we made this observation back in Lesson 5: Be prepared in advance to be asked unexpectedly. If you're attending a special function, ask yourself if you might possibly be asked to "say a few words." If there's any chance of that whatsoever, give some thought in advance to what you'll say if asked. Then you'll be in readiness, and you'll have an outline at hand.

Even if you should find yourself caught off-guard in a public speaking situation, you can still follow these guidelines to make a great speech:

- **Be brief.** Just as practice is important with most types of speeches, so brevity is critical to the impromptu speech. Speaking off the cuff has many pitfalls, not the least of which is the danger of saying something you'll regret. Keep it short and to the point—then sit down.

- **Remember the audience and the setting.** It's likely that you know at least something about the people you're with when asked to deliver an impromptu speech. Before you start speaking, ask yourself what will be appropriate for the audience—and what might be inappropriate.

Select a topic that is pertinent to the occasion, and make the tone match. Humor is appropriate at a celebration, but it must be used with a measure of sensitivity at a memorial service.

- **Make it personal.** That is, personal to you—not to specific members of the audience. People love to hear stories and anecdotes, so draw from your own experience to make an apt illustration. Using someone in the audience as the focus of your story, however, runs a grave risk of offending. Avoid this at all costs!
- **Bite your tongue.** If you're like me, you'll get up unexpectedly to say a few words and suddenly think of a humorous observation on some extraneous topic. I've learned from very painful experience that this can be a deadly trap. I once made a grossly insensitive comment on the food service at a speech location, only to find out later that I'd injured the feelings of a blind person. If only I could have gone back in time and shut my mouth! Remember our favorite maxim: *When in doubt, leave it out.*

Exercise
Use this form to prepare for any type of speech:

Written Speech:
- Write out the speech exactly as you'd like to deliver it, preferably on a computer.
- Read it aloud, paying attention to:
  —awkward wording that sounds stilted or canned
  —places where you would normally gesture or move
  —visual aids that would help
- Make appropriate changes to your speech.
- Read it aloud, noting the same issues.
- Make further changes as required.
- Read it aloud once again.
- Memorize the outline.

Memorized Speech:
- Write out the speech exactly as you'd like to deliver it, preferably on a computer.
- Read it aloud, paying attention to:
  —awkward wording that sounds stilted or canned
  —places where you would normally gesture or move
  —visual aids that would help
- Make appropriate changes to your speech.
- Read it aloud, noting the same issues.
- Make further changes as required.
- Read it aloud once again.
- Memorize the speech by rehearsing it aloud without looking at your manuscript.
- Repeat.
- Repeat again.
- Memorize the outline.

Extemporaneous Speech:
- Create a complete outline from your preliminary outline, preferably on a computer.
- Give the speech aloud, paying attention to:
  —awkward wording that sounds stilted or canned
  —places where you would normally gesture or move
  —visual aids that would help
- Make appropriate changes to your speech.
- Give the speech aloud, noting the same issues.
- Make further changes as required.
- Give the speech once more.
- Print the outline using a large, readable font.

Impromptu Speeches:
- Consider the audience and occasion at which you might be speaking.
- Determine what would be an appropriate:
  —topic
  —tone
  —use of humor or pathos (emotional content)

- Rehearse those thoughts aloud, and imagine how the audience might respond.
- Reword your thoughts to avoid any possibility of offense or inappropriate content.
- Rehearse again.
- Jot pertinent, memory-jogging notes on an index card or scrap of paper.

TIPS

- When reading a speech, make it sound like you're working from an outline.

- When reciting a memorized speech, make it sound like you're making it up on the spot.

- Keep your outline brief. It's a memory-jogger, not a puppet master.

- Practice. Practice some more. Then spend some time practicing. If you get tired of practicing, rehearse for a while.

- Design your printed material for easy reading. This is best done with a computer, *not* with handwritten notes.

11 ▶ SPEAKING RESPONSIBLY

We are here on Earth to do good to others. What the others are here for, I don't know.

—W. H. AUDEN, 1907–1973

LESSON SUMMARY
Everyone is influenced in his or her thinking and ideas by the thinking and ideas of others. It is important to give credit where credit is due, as we'll see in this lesson.

Americans are fiercely protective of the right to free speech, to the point that this right is guaranteed by the very document that defines U.S. government: the United States Constitution. Yet, we must also be aware that the right to free speech carries with it a corresponding expectation that we will use speech responsibly. The right to freedom of speech, for example, may technically include the right to randomly scream "Fire!" in a crowded movie theater. But that does not make such speech a good idea. In fact, to use speech in this way would be incredibly careless, as it would cause unnecessary panic and potential chaos.

Similarly, your opportunity to speak before an audience carries with it a weight of responsibility. An invitation to speak at a conference does not give you the freedom to stand up and tell lies; on the contrary, the people who invited you to speak did so because they trust you to tell the truth. Therefore, we should spend a little time considering the responsibility of a public speaker.

Tell the Truth

The foremost rule is the one we've already suggested: Tell the truth. This probably seems self-evident, but its implications are more wide-ranging than you might expect. In fact, most of the principles covered in this lesson can be summarized under this overall notion.

The first application of this principle is to strive for accuracy. This means that you will want to do broad research before starting your outline. It is not enough to read one or two books or journal articles on your topic; you need to gather information from numerous sources. This ensures that your information is accurate and precise, and not the viewpoints of a single source.

It also requires that you take good notes, as we discussed in previous lessons. If you want to quote an author, you must be certain that you are quoting *exactly* what was written. It's an easy temptation to fudge it by quoting someone as best you can recall without bothering to look it up again, but this is dishonest. If you can't relocate something you want to quote, let your audience know that it's not a direct quotation: "Mark Twain once said something along the lines of. . . ." It's really quite easy to be honest.

Present All Sides to an Argument

This is another element of honesty in public speaking. This principle holds true in all types of speeches, but is most profound in the persuasive speech. The goal of the persuasive speech, after all, is to prove that your opinion is correct and persuade the audience to embrace your opinion—so it can be very tempting to strengthen your argument by ignoring data that contradicts it.

Ironically, by ignoring contradictory information, you will actually weaken your argument in the long run, rather than strengthen it. It is almost certain that someone in your audience will be familiar with such information; and if they don't know it while you're speaking, they will undoubtedly learn it later. This signals to your listeners that you are being dishonest with them, and that is an absolute guarantee of losing their trust.

Conversely, you can actually strengthen your argument by presenting contradictory information. First, it demonstrates to your audience that you have done your research completely, not simply drawing from sources that are in agreement with you, and it reassures them that you are trying to be straightforward in your presentation. This will gain you more credibility and make your listeners more likely to consider your viewpoints.

But one of the best advantages of presenting contradictory information is that it forces you to refine your own viewpoints. It is possible that you'll find some startling information you'd never considered before, thereby reassessing your own opinion on the matter. If that information does not sway your opinion, it will make you ask yourself why—and when you answer the question of why that information is not enough to change your opinion, you will know how to refute it in your speech.

A good persuasive speech does just that: It presents a counterargument from a source that holds a different opinion, and then explains to the audience why that information cannot change the truth of your basic thesis. And all of this is simply part of being honest in your speech.

Do Not Plagiarize

Plagiarism is the crime of taking someone else's work and claiming it as your own. Note my wording here: It's a *crime*. That means that this is not merely an issue of being responsible or ethical; this is an issue of obeying the law. It's the reason that we have copyright protections on books, recordings, film, and many other media—because plagiarism is stealing.

There is another side to this issue that many fail to recognize: Pretending material is yours is lying. This, of course, takes us back to the first principle, and it will destroy any speaker's credibility—sometimes permanently—to be caught in the act.

This applies to "borrowed" material as well as that which is outright stolen from another source. Borrowed material includes canned speeches that are free to use by anyone. You could probably find such sample speeches on the Internet or from books in the library. In this case, you are not breaking any laws by giving those speeches, since the author has given permission for anyone to use them. But you would be breaking a higher law by presenting that speech as though it were your own—the law of trust. (These principles, incidentally, apply just as much to written essays as they do to verbal speeches.)

Finally, plagiarism also includes using visual aids or printed material without crediting where you got it. (Of course, if you create your own, this does not apply.) If you're using PowerPoint slides in your presentation that you downloaded from the Internet, for example, be sure to credit the source. This can be done by writing it directly on the slide, or by stating where you got the slide during your presentation.

Here are the things you'll need to include when citing a printed source:

- Author's name
- Title of work cited
- Publisher, including publisher's location
- Copyright date
- Page number, if appropriate

Here is what you need if citing something found on the Internet:

- Complete URL
- Title of website
- Title of specific work within the website
- Date when you viewed it

Here are samples:

Printed Hand-Out:

This material is quoted from John Smith, *How to Paint Realistic Miniature Figures* (New York: Mini Painting Guild, 2010), 215.

PowerPoint Slide:

From John Smith, *How to Paint Realistic Miniature Figures* (New York: Mini Painting Guild, 2010), 215.

Oral Quotation:

"As John Smith memorably stated in his book *How to Paint Realistic Miniature Figures*, 'Paint selection is the lifeblood of any painting project. Selecting the wrong paint for your project is like eating poison—bad paint can kill your favorite figure.'"

The thing to realize is that crediting your sources actually works in your favor. It enables your audience to recognize that you've done your research, and it builds their confidence in your credibility. And it's so easy to do! Just tell the audience whom you're quoting, and move on. That's all that is asked.

Exercise

Use this questionnaire to determine what sources you need to cite:

- Where in my speech am I quoting directly from someone else?
- Where have my ideas been strongly influenced by someone else?
- Which of my ideas and conclusions are the product of my own thinking?
- How well do I clarify the sources of these three categories of information?
- What visual aids or handouts have I borrowed from another source?
- Use the previous lists to fill out complete citation information on any material that you have drawn from in your speech.

TIPS

- Plagiarism is stealing—and it's against the law!

- Borrowing can be stealing when it's not properly credited.

- Presenting many sides to an issue actually strengthens your case, even when information contradicts your opinion.

- You will not need full citation information (publisher, copyright date, page number, etc.) in a speech, but you still need to have it written down.

- Resist the temptation to use canned material. Learning to write your own material can be hard work, but it's a skill you need to develop.

12 ▶ EMPOWERING YOUR SPEECH

The ill and unfit choice of words wonderfully obstructs the understanding.

—FRANCIS BACON, 1561–1626

LESSON SUMMARY

Rhetoric is the art of using words to communicate ideas. In this lesson, we will learn how to accomplish this more forcefully.

If you have tried reading a complete speech aloud, you have already discovered that word choices are important. Words that read well on the page, for example, may not speak well out loud. Similarly, a well-worded sentence can transform an ordinary statement into something extraordinary and memorable.

Good writing is a skill, and like any other skill it comes only by practice. As you rehearse your speech, pay attention to your choices of words and ask yourself whether you might be able to say things with more punch, as well as more succinctly, accurately, and memorably. After all, you want your audience to remember what you say, and there are many ways in which you can craft your wording to help them remember.

The techniques used to make speeches memorable are called *rhetorical devices*. They are devices or techniques used to enliven *rhetoric*. Rhetoric is the art of using language to persuade, which is at the heart of public speaking. There are many useful rhetorical devices that can keep your audience listening to your words, but we will focus only on the major categories in this lesson.

Spoken Words versus Written Words

We have already touched upon this distinction, but it is worth considering in more detail. A college essay will generally strive for a fairly formal tone, sounding somewhat stiff but erudite. That tone, however, will not sit well with your audience if you try it out in a speech. Your audience wants you to speak to them in a fairly conversational tone, not as though you were reading from an encyclopedia.

This is not to say that your tone will be informal. It might be, depending upon the setting; some special occasions call for a very informal style, such as proposing a toast at a wedding. More frequently, however, you will want your words to be carefully crafted to sound professional while still presenting the information at a level that is suitable to the audience.

You have probably been taught in college writing classes that you should never refer to yourself in an essay, using the first person pronoun *I*. This is appropriate for written essays, but not for spoken speeches. An effective public speaker connects with his or her audience, and the best way to do this (as we've mentioned numerous times) is to draw from your own experiences. You will, therefore, want to refer to yourself directly from time to time during your speech.

Another important aspect of formal writing is to avoid repetition—but this is not the case in a speech. Quite the contrary, in fact. You'll remember our little axiom from Lesson 9: "Tell them what you're going to tell them; tell them; tell them what you told them." Now *that's* repetitive! Yet that sort of repetition is important in a speech, because absorbing information from a lecture is an entirely different process than when one is reading it. You can always flip back a few pages to re-read something in a book, but you can't do that when listening to a speech, so you'll actually be helping your audience if you reiterate your points as you go along.

Alliteration, Repetition, Sequence

Another useful technique to help your audience remember your main points it to use alliteration, the poetic technique of using words that begin with the same letter. The tongue-twister "Peter Piper picked a peck of pickled peppers" uses alliteration, where all the important words in the sentence start with *P*. If your main points all start with the same letter, your audience is far more likely to remember them. Let's return to our toothpaste speech: we could name our major points "Cavities," "Cleansing," and "Cost." All three start with *C*, yet their names allow the listener to remember the gist of what you are saying at each point.

Alternatively, you could use repetition to name your major points. For example, let's return to our miniature painting speech. We could name the three major points in that speech as follows: Paint Selection; Paint Brushing; Paint and Your Miniature. This repetition of the word *paint* ties each point back to the topic, while also encapsulating the information of each one.

Finally, you can name your points in sequence, either numerical or alphabetical. For example, in the toothpaste speech we could name the points "Antiseptic," "Brightening," and "Cost"—*A, B, C*. This provides a mnemonic, or a memory-jogger, for the audience as they recall the major differences between the two toothpastes.

Metaphors and Similes

Another useful technique is the use of metaphors and similes. Both are comparisons between two things that are not typically associated with one another—where you show your audience how they actually *are* associated in some way, thus illustrating your principle.

A simile uses *like* or *as* to draw the comparison, thus showing that the items are *similar* in some way:

"My love is like a rose as it opens to your beauty, shining like the morning sun." This is a simile, because it suggests that love is similar to a rose, using the word *like* to draw the comparison. A metaphor, on the other hand, does not say that love is *like* a rose, but rather that love *is* a rose: "My love is a rose, fragrant and soft."

Metaphors and similes must serve a function in your speech, however. You don't want to use them just to show off; they need to further your audience's understanding of some point that you're trying to make. We used a metaphor in our painting speech: "Paint selection is the lifeblood of any painting project." This helps your audience understand that paint selection is what makes a miniature come to life, and when it's done incorrectly the entire project can wither and die.

Clichés

Clichés should be avoided like the plague. Instead, think outside the box, because what goes around comes around. Been there, done that! No harm, no foul—my bad.

Whenever a speaker tells me to "think outside the box," I immediately recognize that he or she *isn't*. Clichés are the habit of the lazy speaker, the person who won't take the time and effort to think up his or her own words. Some time ago, I heard a speaker say, "Generally speaking, what it boils down to in the final analysis. . . ." This was a triple whammy, three tired out phrases strung together into one dull cliché that didn't communicate anything to the audience.

Now every rule has its counterpart, as we've said before, and clichés are no exception. There are times when a commonly used expression can summarize your point with strong emphasis—but only when you acknowledge that it's a commonly used expression that

has become a cliché. "The label on toothpaste B claims that it fights cavities, and we're commonly told to 'think outside the box.' But in this case, we need to *think inside the tube*!" In this sentence, the speaker used a tired cliché and turned it around with a fresh new meaning that applied directly to the comparison of toothpastes.

Active Voice versus Passive Voice

This is a nitpicky grammatical issue that may not seem very important, but it does make a big difference in your speech. It has to do with how we use verbs, those common action words that we use everyday, such as *walk*, *sit*, and *run*. The active voice states who is doing the action, while the passive voice does not.

- **Active:** "Bill shut the door."
- **Passive:** "The door was shut."

Use of the passive voice tends to make a speech sound vague and indecisive, while the active voice makes it clear that the speaker knows exactly what he or she is talking about. Notice the subtle difference between these two sentences:

- The brochures should all be updated.
- The marketing department should update all the brochures.

In the first example, the speaker has merely suggested a possible idea, while the second example outlines a clear plan that specifically states who should do what. This approach sounds far more authoritative, suggesting to the audience that the speaker has thought through the issue in great detail—even though the essential information is the same!

What to Avoid

Finally, remember that these rhetorical devices are the spices; they are not the main course. Like any other spice, they can be easily overused, making the speech unpalatable to your audience. Resist the temptation of overusing them.

For example, alliteration is useful in naming your main points, but you don't want to get carried away by filling each point with alliterations. Metaphors and similes help your audience to draw mental pictures of the abstract points you're making, but too many metaphors become confusing. Repetition helps the audience remember your speech, but too much repetition will put them to sleep.

The goal of rhetoric is to communicate your ideas effectively to the audience, not to impress them with your skills as a speaker. Never let the devices draw attention to themselves; their job is to draw attention to your ideas, not to stand out on their own.

Exercise

Use this questionnaire to brainstorm ways of spicing up your speech:

- Name your major points using:
  - Alliteration, starting each point with the same letter
  - Sequence, naming them in numerical or alphabetical order
  - Repetition of some word or phrase

- Find a metaphor or simile for each major point:
  - This idea is like _____.
  - This example is comparable to

    _____.

- Look for clichés:
  - Does this cliché really summarize my thoughts?
  - How can I reword this more accurately?
  - Can I turn this cliché around and use it in a fresh new way?

- Keep your voice active:
  - Do my words state clearly who will do what?
  - Have I been vague on any points, leaving things unclear or unstated?

- Don't over-spice:
  - How many metaphors and similes have I used throughout my speech?
  - Do my rhetorical devices help to communicate my ideas, or are they just showy?

TIPS

- Metaphors make an abstract idea more concrete, drawing a comparison between an idea and a real-life example.

- The active voice communicates authority and knowledge, while the passive voice suggests uncertainty. "Smith shot Brown" is more convincing than "Brown was shot."

- Give your major sub-points memorable names to help your audience remember your ideas.

- Alliteration: words that start with the same letter.

- Resist the temptation to use canned material. Learning to write your own material can be hard work, but it's a skill you need to develop.

- Repetition: using a word or phrase repeatedly in each sub-point.

- Sequence: naming your sub-points in a way that emphasizes their position in relation to one another.

- Clichés are for lazy speakers. Find your own way of saying it.

- Clichés *can* be used effectively if you turn them around in a way that delivers a fresh new meaning.

- All rhetorical devices should enhance your communication, not draw attention to themselves.

13 ▶ IN THE EYE OF THE BEHOLDER

The world is governed more by appearance than realities so that it is fully as necessary to seem to know something as to know it.

—DANIEL WEBSTER, 1782–1852

LESSON SUMMARY

A good speech is made up of more than just words; our bodies communicate at least as loudly as our voices. In this lesson, we will learn how to communicate with the whole body.

Never judge a book by its cover, we're told, because appearances can be deceiving. These sayings are very true, of course, yet like all our other rules, they have a counterpart. When it comes to public speaking, your appearance can be as important as your words.

Good grooming and appropriate attire are only a small part of this topic. You can be as tastefully dressed and carefully groomed as a professional and still undermine your message by something as subtle as poor posture or unclear delivery. Let's consider some of the things that go into making a good appearance.

Good Grooming

We'll start with the most obvious area, our physical appearance. It is important to dress in a manner that is appropriate to the occasion. Remember the rule we established in Lesson 9: Always dress one notch better than your audience. Here are some general categories to help you show up with the right amount of style:

- Casual: Jeans, tennis shoes, t-shirts
- Business Casual: Khakis, slacks, casual shirts and blouses, loafers
- Business Formal: Suits, dresses, dress shoes, neckties
- Formal: Tuxedoes, formal gowns, matching accessories

If your audience will be those present at a business meeting on casual Friday, you should plan on dressing in the business formal category. This is just a rule of thumb, however; common sense still applies. You wouldn't address a business audience wearing a top hat and tuxedo.

It's also a good idea to check your facial appearance in a mirror prior to speaking. This will ensure that your hair is in place, there's no spinach in your teeth, and you haven't sneezed out an unwelcome surprise. It will also increase your confidence and decrease your anxiety to know that you don't have to worry about your appearance.

Avoid distracting items such as jangling jewelry or loud colors. I recently sat through an entire lecture staring at the speaker's red tie because I couldn't get over thinking that his tongue was hanging out of his shirt. Bracelets that rustle and make noise are a major distraction whenever you gesture, and even jingling loose change in your pockets can be annoying to the audience.

Good Posture

When I was in elementary school, teachers were constantly admonishing some student or other—frequently me—to stand up straight. There are many reasons for maintaining good posture: Standing erect helps you breathe more comfortably, prevents fatigue, allows you to make eye contact with your audience, and projects your voice better, among other things. But one major reason for good posture is that it projects the image that you are confident and well prepared.

Closely associated with good posture is the notion of "opening out" toward your audience. By this I mean that you face your audience directly, keeping your head up and your eyes at their level, psychologically removing any barrier between you and your listeners and opening up your countenance to them. This is important because it makes your voice project clearly, and it also sends subtle body-language signals to your audience telling them that you are confident and trustworthy.

Of course, like anything else, erect posture can be overdone. You don't need to stand with your chin pressed into your neck and shoulders pushed way back like a Marine—unless you're a Marine. Your goal is to stand comfortably but upright. I have a tendency, evidently, to slump slightly forward and look down. I say "evidently" because I frequently catch myself while speaking in that posture and must consciously remember to square up my shoulders and open out toward the audience. Your best bet is to stand comfortably and remind yourself to keep your face open toward the audience.

Eye Contact

Making good eye contact provides you with one of the most powerful methods of connecting with your audience. It simply involves looking at your listeners—straight into their eyes.

This is a natural habit for most people in normal social conversation. It is instinctive to look into the eyes of a person to whom you are speaking because you gain information that way. We go beyond the words of others in conversation by searching their eyes to find whether they are telling the truth, how they feel emotionally about what they're saying, and whether they're paying attention to us or to their surroundings. The same information is conveyed between you and your audience via sustained eye contact.

Remember to look directly at specific people in the audience as you're speaking, holding their gaze for approximately five seconds, then moving on to make eye contact with someone else. Shift your focus to different parts of the audience, looking at someone on your right, then at someone on your left, and then at someone in the back, and so forth. You'll probably also glance down at your notes from time to time, but this entire process of eye movement also contributes to using motion in your favor.

Good eye contact allows your audience to connect with you, but it also enables *you* to connect with *them*. It lets you know how your listeners are reacting to your words, and it also gives you good information on what parts of your speech are effective and what parts are less so. This information will prove valuable in future speeches, as you learn what works and what doesn't. And if you notice that your audience is dozing off or is distracted, you can make adjustments to your delivery and timing on the spot.

Gestures and Motion

You've undoubtedly heard television newscasters referred to as "talking heads." And, from an audience perspective, that's pretty much what they amount to. The reason is that the newscasters are sitting passively behind a desk, staring straight into the camera, and talking. That is *not* what you want to do when you speak publicly.

Physical motion is an important asset in holding the audience's attention. People naturally look at things that are moving, while we tend to lose interest quickly in stationary objects. You can use that knowledge to your advantage by giving your listeners something to attract their eyes.

Simple hand gestures can be very effective in this regard. Beginning speakers frequently wonder what to do with their hands when they stand in front of an audience, particularly if there is no podium—and here is the answer: Use them to your advantage by making natural gestures as you speak. Following are some tips:

- **Use gestures to emphasize your words.** If you're speaking of an increase in something, use your hands to expand away from each other in an increasing gesture—and vice versa if you're discussing a decrease in something.
- **Use the same gestures you would naturally use when speaking to a friend.** For example, if you said to a friend, "There are three reasons for this," you would probably hold up three fingers. "There is no way I'm doing that" would be accompanied by a palm-outward wave. These same gestures should be used when speaking to an audience.

- **Go with your gut.** If you're getting excited about your topic, let your hands reflect that excitement. If you're showing that your opponent's viewpoints make no sense, let your shoulders shrug up and hands move outward in the familiar "hey, I don't get it either" gesture. Your emotional reactions to your own speech—other than simple nervousness—are good indications of where gestures are needed.
- **Use short, simple gestures.** There are two reasons for this: You don't want to be thinking about your gestures rather than your speech, and you don't want the gestures to become distracting.
- **Don't get carried away.** As with all the other techniques being considered in these lessons, gestures can be overdone. Some people tend to gesture quite freely when they speak in normal conversation, and such habits can actually work against them instead of in their favor. We'll discuss distracting habits in more detail in Lesson 15; for now, be aware that gestures are like any other spice—best used sparingly.

Control Your Voice

This last element is as much a part of your body language as all the other components we've covered. If you mumble and don't project your voice, it tells the audience that you are unsure of what you're talking about. If you bellow like a bull, it tells your listeners that you are angry and confrontational. Both extremes are undesirable.

Learning to project confidently without shouting takes some practice, and the level of your projection will be dramatically influenced by the environment in which you are speaking. If you find yourself in a large hotel conference room, for example, you'll need to speak loudly and clearly to be heard by the people in the back. On the other hand, if you have a microphone, you'll want to moderate back on volume, lest you blast the people in the front.

The key to voice control ties back to Lesson 2: *listening*. Listen to the sound of your own voice as you speak in every situation, noting whether it seems to fill the space or simply sound muffled. Acoustics of rooms vary greatly, and the added dimension of microphone amplification will require that you pay attention to how your voice is reacting to the environment.

Finally, be mindful of your enunciation, making an effort to pronounce your words accurately and clearly. If you have a tendency to speak fast, slowing down will help you to carefully pronounce every syllable in your words. If you have a soft voice, deliberately increasing your volume will help you to enunciate. The goal is to avoid slurring syllables together in individual words.

Exercise

Use a video camera to record a dress rehearsal of your speech; then use this questionnaire to evaluate your delivery:

- Grooming:
  - ❑ Were my clothes appropriate for the audience I'll be addressing?
  - ❑ Was there anything in my appearance that was distracting?
  - ❑ Did I fidget with clothing, jewelry, eyeglasses, etc.?

- Posture:
  - ❑ Was I standing straight?
  - ❑ Was I comfortable?
  - ❑ Was I opened out toward the camera, or was my face obscured at times?

- Eye Contact:
  - ❑ Did I connect with the camera?
  - ❑ If I'd been in the audience, would I have felt connected to the speaker?
  - ❑ Was I heavily dependent on my notes, or free to gaze into the camera?

- Gestures and Motion:
  - ❑ Did I use my hands effectively?
  - ❑ Did my gestures become a distraction?
  - ❑ Did I move my body, or stand like a frozen statue?

- Voice:
  - ❑ How well did I project my voice?
  - ❑ Did I speak clearly?
  - ❑ Did I enunciate my words well, or did I tend to slur at times?

TIPS

- Remember to enunciate. Practice by saying this sentence out loud, clearly enunciating each syllable: *"Re-mem-ber to e-nunc-i-ate."*

- Don't fidget with your clothing, jewelry, eyeglasses, etc. In general, keep your hands away from your face.

- Moving away from the podium to the left or right can be effective, but be careful not to overdo it. Too much movement is as distracting as too little.

- Stand comfortably, but stand straight.

- Make eye contact with individuals for approximately five seconds.

- Move your eyes over the entire audience; don't focus solely on those people in the middle.

14 ▶ SEEING IS BELIEVING

A picture is worth a thousand words.
—ANONYMOUS

LESSON SUMMARY

Listening to someone speak is an effective way of learning, but you can add the element of visual aids to your speech to enhance the learning experience. This lesson will show you what to do-and what to avoid doing.

Good speaking is more than words, as we've said numerous times already. One nonverbal element of a good speech is the use of visual aids. Visual elements are important for several reasons. First, they grab your audience's attention. Second, they allow your listeners to use their eyes as well as their ears. Third, visual aids reinforce your ideas by providing concrete examples of abstract principles.

Visual aids refers to just about anything your audience can see. This can include those negative visual aspects we've discussed in previous lessons, such as a loud necktie (we'll take a closer look at visual distractions in the next lesson), as well as anything tangible that helps the audience better understand your words.

Objects

One of the most effective forms of visual aid is a three-dimensional object. Demonstrative speeches practically require objects to be effective, as you will want to demonstrate whatever you're talking about. A speech on how to repair a computer, for example, ought to include a real-life computer for demonstration.

But objects are not restricted to demonstrative speeches by any means. When you were a child, you undoubtedly had teachers who gave "object lessons," lessons that taught some abstract principle using a real-life object as an illustration. This is a very powerful speech technique, and it should not be limited to children. Here are some ways that you can add objects to your speech:

- **Make it pertinent to your point.** Simply holding up some random object is not the goal here. Your visual aid must advance your speech in some way. A clock might be useful in a speech on the history of time-keeping, but it might not be helpful in a speech on present tax rates.
- **Make the connection clear to your audience.** Your visual aid might seem completely unrelated to your topic (which doesn't really contradict our previous point). For example, you might in fact use a clock as a visual aid in a speech on current tax rates—*if* you clearly connect it to your topic by turning back the clock as you speak about returning tax rates to a former time period.
- **Make sure the audience can clearly see your visual aid.** Your "turn back the hands of time" idea in using a clock will only be effective if the audience can see the hands moving backward.
- **Make it interactive.** Simply holding up a clock while speaking about turning back time is far less effective than actually interacting with the clock, such as by making the hands move in reverse.

Maps, Charts, Graphs

A traditional method of adding visuals to a speech is to use large printed materials. These can still be very effective tools today, providing a great deal of technical information in an easily understood visual format.

Maps are useful whenever you are speaking about a geographical region, because they help your audience see visually where the region is in relation to themselves. Charts and graphs can take abstract information and make it come alive, showing trends, percentages, numerical relationships, and so on, in colorful detail.

The downside to these traditional methods is that they tend to be fairly labor intensive. You might be familiar with the traditional "flip chart," which is essentially a huge pad of blank paper that you can flip through, page by oversized page. The difficulty is that these pages are *blank*, which means you need to fill them with your own visual aids, drawing charts and graphs by hand. It might be simpler to create such aids on a computer or to download them off the Internet beforehand.

Follow these tips when using traditional methods:

- **Make sure the audience can clearly see your aids.** You might need to get an easel to prop them up, and you might even be forced to elevate the easel on a stage or riser. Seat yourself at the very back of the room to find out how difficult it will be to see your visual aids.
- **Explain them to your audience.** This is especially true of any types of graph or chart that have multiple things going on. For example, a pie chart showing percentages of income from various sources will need to be explained, pointing out each slice of the pie and explaining what it represents. When using maps, point out where your audience is on the map and where the area is that you're discussing.

- **Avoid clutter.** This is the corollary to the previous principle. It might be tempting to cram all your information into one flow chart—especially if you have to create it by hand—but that can be counterproductive. Keep the charts simple, and use multiple charts to cover lots of information.
- **Do not stand in front of your aids.** This is especially problematic with these traditional forms of visual aids, because you will want to point out elements of each one as you speak. Your temptation will be to face the chart to find the things you want to discuss, then remain standing in front of it with your back to the audience. Don't do this. Turn to face them while keeping your finger or pointer in place.

Blackboards and Whiteboards

An even more traditional method of using visual aids is the blackboard and its modern counterpart, the whiteboard. The benefit of these is that you will be able to create your visual aids while speaking, drawing, or writing on the board. Of course, this is also the big downside, since you can't prepare your material in advance.

Even so, drawing while you speak is a great way to rivet your audience's attention, and writing out pertinent points as you go helps make abstract information more concrete. Follow the principles listed for maps and charts when using a blackboard or whiteboard.

Slides

There was a time when a slide projector was considered indispensable to any public speaking forum. It enabled a speaker to show visual images of almost anything he or she wanted to talk about, whether a trip to exotic locales or colorful pie charts and graphs. It enabled the audience to see visuals clearly, since even something like a tiny watch gear could be photographed and enlarged to clear visibility.

The advent of digital photography, however, has changed all this, and these days it might be difficult to ever get your hands on a carousel slide projector. Yet, you might find yourself in a situation that demands a slide projector, such as needing to use 35mm photographs to illustrate your presentation. (Even in that situation, incidentally, you might do better to have the images scanned into digital format and use a PowerPoint projector.) If you do need a slide projector, follow these tips:

- **Be sure that the room can be darkened enough for the slides to be visible.** This is one of the downsides to slides: A darkened room invites your audience to take a nap. But the slides won't be visible if there is extraneous light; you might even need to cover windows.
- **Do not move through the slides too quickly—or too slowly.** You should leave each slide on screen for approximately 20 seconds to allow your audience to examine it. More than that runs the risk of becoming boring, while less makes the viewer's eyes spin.
- **Use a remote control.** When I was growing up, slide projectors didn't have carousels; each slide was "injected" and "ejected" by a side-to-side sliding mechanism. The speaker would stand at the front and say "next," while an assistant operated the projector. This created a very sleepy cadence that never failed to lull me into a nap. A remote allows you to move through the slides at your own pace without interruption.

Overheads

The overhead projector was considered state of the art when I was young, but these days it has been supplanted by PowerPoint presentations. All the same, I still like to use it when possible for a number of reasons.

For one thing, an overhead projector gives you great flexibility. You can order your transparencies however you want them, and then reorder them on the fly as needed. You can have a mixture of prepared transparencies and blank ones to write on as you speak. (In the olden days, projectors even had rolls of transparency material stretched across them so you could write to your heart's content, scrolling as you went along.)

Follow these tips when using an overhead projector:

- **Number your transparencies.** They are slippery, and sooner or later you will drop them. Trust me on this. It is most likely to happen just as you are about to use them, and then it's too late to put them back in order. Numbers discreetly written in a corner will be a lifesaver.
- **Look up!** Of all the visual aids we're discussing, the overhead projector is probably the worst for those who get distracted by their aids. You can so easily find yourself standing over the projector, staring down at your transparency as you speak, and this is a real trap.
- **Point to the screen, not to the transparency.** This principle grows out of the previous one. The reason that you'll be staring down is that you'll be pointing out details in your transparency to your audience. Instead, use a pointer of some sort (a yardstick will do if you don't have a laser pointer) to indicate what you're discussing directly on the screen. And remember to face your audience rather than the screen, as we've discussed already.
- **Prepare the projector *before* you speak.** Overheads need to be adjusted for audience visibility in more ways than other projectors. You need to position them the correct distance from the screen to get the largest image possible; you need to swivel the mirror head to the center of the screen (and also to

minimize the keystone effect); and you need to focus the mirror head up and down. All this requires your full attention on the projector, and will seriously interfere with your speech. Do it ahead of time so you won't have to think about it when speaking.

PowerPoint

This computer-based application has become the industry standard in presenting visual aids, replacing most of the two-dimensional approaches we've discussed thus far. (Nothing can ever quite replace a compelling use of three-dimensional objects.) PowerPoint enables you to create visually attractive slides that present information in almost any format you desire. If you're computer savvy, you can even incorporate motion and sound into your presentation.

The downside to PowerPoint is, ironically, the very fact that it is so powerful and easy to use. Many speakers become overly dependent upon their PowerPoint presentations and forget to develop their speech properly. This can lead to a speech that is more of a slide show than a public speaking event. As with all other visual aids, your PowerPoint presentation exists solely to further your speech—not vice versa.

Follow these tips when using PowerPoint:

- **Do not read your slides to the audience.** They can read; let them. Use the words on a slide to augment the words you speak, or to give a broad overview of a point while you go into greater depth verbally.
- **Use visual images in your slides effectively.** Colors and clip art can enhance the words on a slide and make them more interesting to look at. But the rules for objects apply here, too: Graphic images should have some connection to the words. Don't overdo animations or other graphic effects. They are a visual spice; use them sparingly.

- **Use a legible font.** Computers make it tempting to play around with fancy fonts, such as pretty scripts and unusual specialty fonts. But those fancy fonts can be very difficult to read from the back of an audience, causing your visual aids to become visual distractions. When in doubt, use Times New Roman—and remember to make it large enough to read from far away.

- **Have someone proofread your slides.** I can't tell you how many times I've sat through PowerPoint presentations that were filled with typos and misspellings. This does more than distract the audience; it makes the speaker look careless and unprepared! Do not depend on your computer's spell-check feature, either, since it will not catch the most flagrant spelling errors—such as *to, too,* and *two*; *women* instead of *woman*; *their, they're,* and *there*; and many other common mistakes.

Handouts

Finally, printed sheets of paper can be an effective form of visual aid. In fact, they are one of the most effective forms, because they give the audience information they can literally take home with them. There is also a tactile element to a printed sheet of paper, something the audience can touch and feel, which is not available in a slide presentation.

Follow these tips when handing out printed material:

- **Keep it brief.** As with all visual aids, avoid the pitfall of putting too much information into your handouts. An outline works well, or bulleted points like the lists in this book. These are just short sentences and phrases that summarize the information that you have expounded on in your speech.

- **Keep it simple.** Don't fall prey to the temptation to show off your fonts and clip art. Stick to the reason for the handout and avoid extraneous elements that will distract a reader.

- **Keep it until the end.** The danger of handouts is that you cannot make your audience stop looking at them. Slides are an advantage in that respect; when you're done, you turn it off. But once you give your listeners something to read, they become readers rather than listeners. Don't distribute handouts until you're done speaking.

The Cardinal Rules for Visual Aids

No matter what you use to spice up your speech, remember these important principles:

- **They're called aids for a reason.** The purpose of a visual aid is to assist you in your speech. Don't let them become the center of attention; use them to further your points, then put them away.

- **Don't get distracted.** Many speakers become absorbed in their own visual aids, staring at them intently while they speak, even speaking to the aid rather than to the audience. If you get distracted, so will your listeners. Pay attention to the audience, not to the visual aids.

- **It must be clearly visible to everyone.** Make sure that your object is large enough for all to see and understand what you're doing with it. Check visibility of the screen from the farthest corners of the room. If you're talking about something that someone can't see, that person will not be listening to your words.

- **Keep it relevant!** Remember the first point in this list—it's an aid to your presentation, not something to entertain the audience. Make sure you clearly explain how your visual aids relate to your topic.

Exercise

Use this questionnaire to select and analyze your visual aids:

■ What analogies or metaphors best explain my main points?

_____

_____

■ What media will best help me make visual pictures of these analogies?
   ❑ Three-dimensional objects
   ❑ Graphs or pie charts
   ❑ Words that expand on the points

■ Where will I get these items?
   ❑ Something that I own or use on a regular basis
   ❑ Statistics in a spreadsheet that creates pie charts or graphs
   ❑ Images from the Internet

■ What mechanical apparatus will I need to use these aids?
   ❑ Flip chart
   ❑ Overhead projector
   ❑ PowerPoint projector

■ What will I say while showing these visual aids?
   ❑ How does each one explain my major points?
   ❑ What details will I need to explain on each visual aid?

■ How can I simplify?
   ❑ Are my charts and graphs too complicated?
   ❑ Am I incorporating too much information?
   ❑ Will I become dependent on one of these aids rather than on my words?

TIPS

- Any visual aid can quickly become a visual distraction. Be on guard against this.

- A visual aid is worthless if your audience can't see it.

- Speak to the audience, not to the visual aid.

- Set up any mechanical devices in advance, such as an overhead projector or easel.

- Keep it simple.

- Explain clearly how each visual aid applies to your overall purpose.

15 ▶ AVOIDING DISTRACTIONS

By prevailing over all obstacles and distractions, one may unfailingly arrive at his chosen goal or destination.

—CHRISTOPHER COLUMBUS, 1451–1506

LESSON SUMMARY

Anything that distracts your audience is working to defeat your speech—even if it's coming from you! In this lesson, we will consider how to avoid some often overlooked distractions.

Throughout our lessons, we have frequently touched upon the danger of distractions. A distraction is anything that turns your audience's attention—or your own—away from your words toward something else. Distractions can come from the environment, as we discussed briefly in Lesson 2. They can come from your presentation, as mentioned regarding visual aids in Lesson 14. And what's most dangerous of all, they can come directly from *you*!

Your job as a public speaker is to help your audience learn something they can apply in their own lives. To do this, you need to be on guard against anything that will interfere with your listeners' learning process. In a sense, you are more than a speaker; you are both a teacher and a guard. You want to teach your listeners about something that is important to you, but you also need to stand guard against outside factors that may prevent their learning.

Um. . . Ah. . . Like. . . You Know. . . See What I Mean?

Most speakers are not even aware of one of the most prominent sources of distraction: verbal mannerisms. I generally find this topic the most difficult to convey to my students, yet it is so pervasive that it cannot be ignored.

Everyone has certain habits of speech that crop up continually in casual conversation. We all tend to say "well . . ." and "ah . . ." when we're trying to find the right words. Yet even in casual conversation, this habit can become distracting. You've probably known someone who says "like" constantly: "I was like walking out of the store, ya know? And she was like standing in my way, like all upset, and I like tried to walk past. . . ." Friends will sometimes tease a person who does this, counting the number of times the filler word is used in a given sentence. This demonstrates the basic fact of such mannerisms: If your audience is counting how many times you say "like," they are *not* listening to the rest of your words!

Filler words are not the only distracting element of speech. Simple intonation of one's voice can become irritating after a while. Perhaps you've had a teacher who droned in monotone throughout his or her lectures; if so, you know how dull and distracting it can be to listen to poor intonation.

A very common problem in this area is known as *upspeak*. Upspeak is the habit of ending sentences—even small phrases—in an upward intonation. To understand this, read the following sentences aloud, noticing how you sound:

- I was walking down the street, when I passed a yellow dog.

- I was walking? Down the street? When I passed? A yellow dog?

Did you hear the upward intonation in your voice as you read the questions? That's the sound of upspeak, ending phrases or sentences on an upward inflection as though you were asking a question, rather than stating a simple fact.

The danger of upspeak is that it conveys to your audience the notion that you are not at all sure of the truth of what you're saying! If you state your information to sound like a question, then the audience feels compelled to wonder what the answer is.

Filler words and vocal intonations convey more to your audience than the words themselves. These habits can be hard to break, but they must be broken if you hope to speak well. The best way to discover your own vocal mannerisms is to video yourself during speech practice. Pay attention to these elements, and then rehearse your speech in front of the camera again, deliberately avoiding those mannerisms. With practice, this avoidance will become a habit.

That Twitch

Physical mannerisms can also be very distracting to your audience. I had a college professor who always had a coffee cup in her hand, which she would rub throughout her lecture as though her hands were freezing cold. When she got excited, she would clink her rings against it. At first, this seemed like a casual approach to teaching—but before long it was simply a distraction. I found myself rubbing my hands together to warm them up, while longing for a steaming cup of java!

There are as many physical mannerisms as there are people in the world, and the best way to discover yours is to watch for them in your practice video, which we discussed previously. Here are some things to be on guard against:

- Fiddling with clothing or jewelry
- Touching your face

- Smoothing your hair
- Rubbing your hands together
- Grabbing your arm or hugging yourself
- Squinting, wriggling your nose, or licking your lips
- Gesturing wildly
- Playing with objects, such as a pen or your notes

There is also the case of a physical distraction you cannot help, such as a disability or incorrigible tic. You have several options in this case. You can make a joke of it if you feel comfortable doing so (and if you can do so without it coming across as forced). You can simply acknowledge it, getting the so-called elephant in the room out of the way. And you can absolutely ignore it if that's what makes you most comfortable. The ultimate goal is to change the focus of the speech to the *message* and your words—not your physical presence.

Nervous Motion

In a previous lesson, we suggested that it's good to move around a bit, rather than stand frozen like a statue. Now, we will consider the other side to that principle: too much movement, or nervous motion.

It can be effective in holding your audience's attention to move out from behind the podium from time to time, but it will become very distracting if you do it too frequently or too far. For example, walking into the audience will rivet your listeners' attention, but you only want to do it once. If you continually walk into the audience, your listeners will begin to anticipate it and will pay more attention to wondering when you'll pay your next visit than they do to your words.

It is much better to walk to your left or right away from the podium, such as moving to use a visual aid. But this, too, can be overdone. Most of your speech should be given from one spot, such as behind the podium.

Nervous motion can also be distracting, such as continually rocking back on your heels or rolling up onto your toes. Some people habitually tap a toe or jiggle their knees; others habitually jingle change in their pockets. These habits will drive your audience to distraction. They won't remember your words, but they will remember how much money you carry around.

The Best Laid Plans

We discussed a number of environmental conditions in Lesson 2 that can become a distraction to your audience, and we made suggestions on how you can minimize or even remove those conditions. But to paraphrase poet Robert Burns, "The best-laid plans of mice and men often go awry." No matter how well prepared you are, something unexpected is almost guaranteed to occur.

Mechanical devices are a frequent source of unwelcome surprises. The battery goes dead on your microphone midway through your speech; you flip on the overhead projector, hear a slight pop, and the bulb goes out; you fire up your PowerPoint presentation, only to discover that you copied the wrong file to your flash drive.

Being human is another source of unexpected entertainment. You lose your place in your notes and suddenly go blank, or you trip on the step up to the stage and fall flat on your face. When I was a graduate student, I was teaching a freshman English class one warm spring day, and things were going great. The students laughed heartily at my witticisms—a trifle more than expected, even—and every eye was riveted on me as I lectured. I had their undivided attention, and I felt quite good about my delivery that afternoon—until a student informed me as she was leaving that my zipper had been down the whole time. Oops. Feel free to not take yourself too seriously—to laugh at yourself, even. We're all human, speaker and audience alike.

There are a million things that can go wrong during a speech, and the only thing you can do is to take it in stride and not lose your composure. Here are a few suggestions on how to handle the unexpected:

- **Ask for help.** You drop your notes or your overhead transparencies, and they scatter across the floor. Don't panic! Calmly ask someone in the front to collect them while you begin or continue speaking.
- **Improvise.** You did memorize your outline, right? Just continue discussing whatever point you were on, using part of your brain to calmly collect your thoughts on where you'll go next.
- **Make a joke at your own expense.** The audience is actually not hostile, and they're not sitting there hoping that you'll fall on your face. They empathize with the stress of public speaking, and they'll quickly join you in a good laugh—provided that it's at *your* expense! Never lose your cool and blame someone else. I actually did trip on a step going up to the stage once, and dropped my notes to boot. I collected my papers, walked to the podium, caught my breath, and then said, "I meant to do that." It wasn't the greatest witticism ever recorded, but it was sufficient.
- **Carry on and ignore technical problems.** You can always summarize the slide that you'd intended to show if the projector isn't working. The visual aids were only intended to assist your speech anyway, so keep going with the main purpose of your being there—your speech.
- **Act like Abe Lincoln.** He didn't have a microphone, yet he riveted his audience's attention by projecting his voice. You can do the same.
- **Adjust.** Some microphones, for example, are very sensitive to popping, such as when you voice the letter *p*. If you're hearing strange feedback, move back from the microphone or stop using it altogether.
- **Plan ahead.** As already stated, this is not foolproof, but it definitely does help. Arrive early at the speech location and get to know the room and equipment you'll be using. See Lesson 2 for more suggestions. The more you troubleshoot in advance, the fewer surprises you'll encounter.

Exercise

Make a video of your speech, then analyze it for distractions using this questionnaire:

- What verbal mannerisms do I have?

_____

_____

—Which ones might be distracting?

_____

_____

- Do I exhibit any of the following?
  - ❑ Verbal filler words (ah, like, okay, etc.)
  - ❑ Monotone
  - ❑ Repetitive intonation (upspeak, etc.)
  - ❑ Speaking too fast or too slow

- How will I compensate for these tendencies?

  _____

  _____

- What physical mannerisms do I have?

  _____

  _____

  —Which ones might be distracting?

  _____

  _____

- Do I exhibit any of the following?
  - ❑ Touching my face
  - ❑ Fiddling with clothes or jewelry
  - ❑ Hugging myself
  - ❑ Playing with objects, such as notes or a pen
  - ❑ Facial ticks

- What can I do to compensate for these habits?

  _____

  _____

■ What happened that I didn't expect?

_____

_____

—How did I handle it?

_____

_____

—What other things might happen when I actually give the speech?

_____

_____

TIPS

- Keep your hands away from your face.

- Use humor at your own expense, never at someone else's. Take the blame for the unexpected on yourself—even when it's not your fault.

- Don't speak too fast. When in doubt, it's better to speak slowly than quickly.

- Memorize your outline! If all else fails, you can still improvise to get the gist of your speech across.

AVOIDING DISTRACTIONS

16 ▶ OVERCOMING ANXIETY

There are only two types of speakers in the world: 1. The nervous, and 2. Liars.

—MARK TWAIN, 1835–1910

LESSON SUMMARY

Everyone gets nervous before speaking publicly. The secret is not to avoid stage fright, but to use it to your advantage.

You're sitting in the front row of a large auditorium that is crowded with people. A woman is on stage introducing the keynote speaker: *you*! Your stomach is knotting up; your throat is scratchy; you feel sweat trickling down your spine, yet you are inexplicably chilly. What should you conclude from these strange symptoms?

You should conclude that you are normal. Whether you realize it or not, nearly everyone gets nervous before speaking in public. I've been getting up in front of audiences in many different settings for more than 30 years, and I still feel my heart rate increase as the moment draws close. It's such a common phenomenon that it even has a name: stage fright.

Indeed, we can learn a lot about stage fright from those who know it best, professional actors who literally get on stage night after night before a large audience. A professional actor will be quick to tell you that stage fright is a good thing, not a bad thing. It indicates that you want to do well, and that you're taking the performance seriously. A lack of stage fright frequently leads to mediocrity, and actors learn to tap into their nervous energy to enhance their performance. You can, too!

The Fear of Fear Itself

The first and most important skill in overcoming stage fright is to recognize that it is a normal sensation. Even professional public speakers get nervous before standing in front of an audience. When you feel those butterflies warming up in your stomach, remind yourself that it is just part of the process of giving a speech.

What often happens to novice speakers, however, is that they convince themselves that they are nervous for good reason: They're going to fail. That sort of thinking can become a self-fulfilling prophecy. If you remind yourself that everyone gets nervous before speaking, you will actually calm down a bit and your mental focus will shift from your fears to your speech.

When you listen to a skillful speaker, recognize that he or she was nervous before getting to the podium. If others can overcome their fears and perform well, so can you. Stage fright is either too much attention on *self* or even on *audience*. In effective public speaking, the message must eventually transcend the medium.

Pretend to Be Confident

A cardinal rule when speaking publicly is not to tell the audience that you're nervous. You might think that everyone can plainly see your shaking hands or beads of sweat on your brow, but the truth is that they can't. Once again, recall the polished speakers to whom you've listened and ask yourself whether they appeared nervous. They didn't, of course—yet chances are, they were.

Appearing confident sends the audience the message that you are prepared and you know your material well. This makes them confident that you have something worthwhile to say to them, and their confidence in you will actually bolster your confidence in yourself. The opposite, unfortunately, is also true: If you tell the audience that you're nervous, they lose confidence in your speech, which will reinforce your own nervousness.

On the other hand, if you are absolutely certain that you cannot hide the terror on your face or in your body mannerisms, you *might* want to consider, as a last resort, reverting back to the "we're all human" school of thought and make a joke of it. Get the audience to laugh, briefly commiserate, and then once the ice is broken, focus, focus, focus on the message you are hoping to convey.

Here are some things you can do to project an air of confidence:

- **Stand up straight.** We have covered the importance of this already, but here is another side to good posture. If you stand tall, your audience will interpret that as confidence, and it will make you feel more confident as well.
- **Focus and relax beforehand.** Do stretches, breathing exercises, and some kind of meditation or mind-centering on a regular basis to be better prepared.
- **Walk briskly to the podium.** Don't run, just walk with an air of eagerness. You want to communicate the notion that you are eager to start sharing your thoughts with the audience—not that you're eager to get the ordeal over with.
- **Greet your audience with a smile.** This conveys a friendly confidence to your audience, while it actually buys you a few precious moments to catch your breath and adjust your thoughts to your speech. In many cases, the audience will also respond verbally to your greeting, saying "good morning" back! That's another bonus to help you calm your fears.

■ **Do not apologize.** As already stated, the audience is not aware of your stage fright, so don't spoil the illusion by telling them about it unless you feel it is absolutely necessary.

Take a Deep Breath

This technique actually ties closely together with the good posture we've been emphasizing, since posture does influence your physical tension. Standing straight and keeping your head up actually helps to remove some of that tension. There are other things you can do physically that will alleviate anxiety. Here are a few:

■ **Take a walk.** Moving around is a great way of releasing anxiety, so plan on taking a short walk prior to your speech event. Stroll around and explore the building and grounds where you'll be speaking. Make it a leisurely stroll, however; you're not trying to work up a sweat, but merely get the blood flowing.

■ **Talk to people.** Getting to know who's in the audience will greatly reduce your anxiety. It's far easier to speak to someone you know than to a complete stranger. When you get up to speak, you can look for those people with whom you spoke and make eye contact.

■ **Sit comfortably when waiting to be introduced.** Anxiety tends to make us ball up into a knot, so deliberately stretch out your legs and wriggle your toes. Sit with your hands in your lap, not with your arms crossed. And avoid the temptation of cracking your neck. Many people jerk their heads to and fro to release neck tension, but this will only tell the people around you that you're tense.

■ **Squeeze your chair.** This is somewhat the opposite of the previous suggestion, but it can be a good way to channel your tension if

relaxing doesn't help. Discretely grip the edge of your chair and squeeze it tight, focusing your tension into your grip. You can do the same to the podium when you get up to speak. The key here is to be discrete, not to let the audience see your knuckles turn white.

Be Prepared!

The greatest antidote to stage fright is the knowledge that you are well prepared. When you start feeling nervous, simply review in your mind how you intend to open your speech. Visualize how you will walk up front, what you'll do when you get there, and how you intend to engage the audience. These things will reassure you that you are indeed ready, and your anxiety will decrease.

This, of course, ties back to nearly every lesson we've done so far. As I said in Lesson 1, being prepared before you begin will pay off big time when you actually speak! As you listen to yourself being introduced, you will be glad you memorized your outline, glad you rehearsed many times over, and glad you did extensive research—overall, you'll be glad you prepared in advance.

When you're feeling stage fright just prior to speaking, simply refocus your mind away from your anxiety and onto your speech. Remind yourself what you intend to say; review your major points; visualize yourself speaking your opening words—and picture yourself speaking clearly and slowly. When the time actually comes, putting that mental picture into practice will flow like a habit; you'll hardly even think about it.

Remember one final point about stage fright: It mostly disappears the moment you start speaking. As soon as you hit your stride and start getting into the meat of your lecture, you will stop thinking about yourself and your anxiety and focus entirely on your speech. All those hours of practice will now pay off, and nobody will know that you're nervous—because you won't be!

Exercise

Practice these stress-relief techniques in advance so you'll know what to do on the day of your speech:

- Breathing exercises:
  — Take a deep breath, drawing it in slowly through your nose, not your mouth.
  — Hold it for two seconds, then begin releasing it—slowly.
  — Take longer to release the air than it took to inhale.

- Stretching exercises:
  — Sit in a chair, preferably one that promotes good posture—*not* a comfortable recliner-type.
  — Sit up straight, squaring your shoulders.
  — Stretch your legs out in front of you while still keeping your feet flat on the floor.
  — Push your heels into floor, lifting your toes to stretch your calves.
  — Keep your hands in your lap or on your thighs while stretching your arms and shoulders.
  — Wriggle your fingers and toes.

- Walking exercises:
  — Pretend you've just been introduced. Stand up briskly and with confidence.
  — Walk across the room with a confident stride, head up and shoulders back.
  — If possible, visit your speech location early and repeat these exercises.

TIPS

- Channel your anxiety and nervous energy into enthusiasm for your topic.

- Never apologize for being nervous or unprepared. Pretend to be confident, and you'll become confident.

- Don't wriggle your head around to loosen up your neck or shoulders. This is like a neon sign saying, "I'm tense!"

- When stage fright grips you, refocus your thinking to concentrate on the positive aspects of your speech.

- Greet your audience with a smile.

17 ▶ PRACTICE, PRACTICE, PRACTICE!

An ounce of practice is worth more than tons of preaching.

—MAHATMA GANDHI, 1869–1948

LESSON SUMMARY

Nobody ever learned a new skill without practice. The more you rehearse, the stronger your speech will be. In this lesson, we will consider some ways of doing this.

There's a saying in the real estate sales industry: "The three most important factors in selling a house are location, location, and location." The three most important factors for public speaking are practice, practice, and more practice.

We must remember that public speaking is a skill—more specifically, a *learned* skill. It is true that some people are born with talent for the performing arts and some are not, but anyone can learn to speak effectively just as much as anyone can learn to drive a car. The main ingredient of learning any skill is to practice. Simply reading this book will not make you an effective public speaker; you need to *do* it to *learn* it.

Use a Video Camera

If at all possible, use a video camera to tape yourself rehearsing your actual speech. An audio recorder will suffice if you can't get your hands on video, but seeing yourself is infinitely more valuable. You will be delivering the speech in person rather than over the radio, after all, and your audience will clearly see you.

Place the camera on a tripod if you can get one; if not, position it securely atop a table or pile of books. You can also have a friend run the camera, but you do not want it hand-held. The camera needs to be completely stationary so that the entire focus is on you, without any distracting camera motion coming into play. Zoom the lens out enough to see yourself from the top of your head to your waist, but not so far that you can't get a good look at your face.

Ideally, you should make at least two separate videos. The first will be on your first or second pass through the speech. When you watch it, you will mostly pay attention to the content of your speech, looking for places that need strengthening. Subsequent videos will be made as your speech develops. In watching these, you will want to pay more attention to your delivery than to your content.

Try closing your eyes during parts of your second or third video, listening only to your voice. This will help you detect any verbal mannerisms that might be distracting, while also analyzing whether you are using effective voice inflections. Then try watching yourself with the sound turned off, paying attention strictly to your visual presentation.

If you're using slides, PowerPoint, or similar visual aids (other than three-dimensional objects), do not worry about capturing them on the video. You can analyze their effectiveness separately. The video is strictly to assess your own performance, both visually and audibly. (However, you will still want to be including those visual aids when giving your speech, even though the camera is not recording them.)

Live Performance

As your speech becomes more polished, conscript a friend or family member to be your captive audience. (You can do this while videotaping, if necessary.) Speaking to a live audience influences your delivery in subtle but important ways.

You will get a real-time sense of your audience's response as you rehearse this way. You will also get the feel for making eye contact, using visual aids, and setting your delivery cadence when speaking to real people. The more you practice these techniques, the more likely it is that they will become second nature.

Another major value of imposing on friends is to get their reactions. You will get some sense of your effectiveness during your speech, gauging whether they are bored, confused, interested, engaged, and so forth. But the bigger value comes from their critique when you're done.

For this part, you should ask your audience to be harsh! Most people are hesitant to sound judgmental or critical of a friend or family member, and they might not want to tell you truthfully if there was a problem. They will be doing you a great disservice if they hold back, and you should ask them to be as honest and forthright as possible. Give them a copy of the exercise at the end of this lesson and ask them to critique you on it.

One more important step: Have your audience ask questions when you're done. Ask them to be thinking of some challenging questions while you are speaking. This will give you some practice fielding questions, and it will also help you to prepare intelligently for any real-life questions you might be fielding when you give your speech.

Practice on Location

If at all possible, your final practice should be alone in the actual setting of your speech. For example, if you're giving this speech to a public speaking class, go to the classroom when it's empty and rehearse, with or without a camera.

Practice sitting where you'll be seated just prior to speaking. Pretend that you've just been introduced, and walk to the podium or stage. Face your imaginary audience, greet them with a smile, and begin.

This will give you a true sense of all your environmental conditions: the sound responsiveness of the room, the presence or absence of microphone amplification, the lighting and heating, and so forth. It will also give you the chance to rehearse using your visual aids, operating whatever equipment you'll be using, and actually running through the slides, transparencies, charts, and whatever other materials you plan to incorporate into your speech. You will also discover any other items that you might want in your presentation, such as a pointer or an extra table.

The value of practicing on site is inestimable. It allows you to visualize exactly where you'll be standing, to hear just what your voice will sound like, to anticipate where your audience will be sitting, and so forth. It will go a long way to reduce your anxiety, because you'll know in advance what you'll be facing.

Rest Time

If you've crammed for your speech, you'll be exhausted when you actually deliver it—and that will not help you in any way! It is vital to have some time off from your speech before delivering it for a number of reasons. First, it allows your mind to rest from the topic, dealing with other real-life issues that might have been put on the back burner during preparation. And it's interesting how your mind will continue mulling over the speech when you're not consciously thinking about it; you might even find yourself beefing up some of your points as a result.

Another important reason for rest is that your delivery will improve if you are not tired. Your mind will be sharp and focused, ready to handle any questions that the audience might throw at you, and you will able to think more quickly on your feet if something unexpected occurs. Your body will not be tense and anxious, and your movements will be smooth and natural.

But in order to get some time off, you'll need to start early! You should have your speech completely prepared *at least* 24 hours before you deliver it. This will give you a full day of freedom from preparation, allowing you to turn your mind and body to other activities, which will recharge your emotional batteries. I like to do something completely different, particularly something involving physical exercise, on the day before a speech. I try to get outside and get some fresh air, taking a walk on the beach or doing yard work. When I get up on the morning of the speech, I take an hour to go through my notes and rehearse my introduction and first point one last time. Then I stop thinking about it until the actual time arrives.

And all of these techniques take us back to our previous lesson: Being well prepared reduces stage fright, and reduced anxiety improves your performance.

Exercise

Give this questionnaire to your rehearsal audience, along with the questionnaire in Lesson 18:

- How was my physical appearance during my speech? Was I:
  - ❑ appropriately dressed?
  - ❑ properly groomed?
  - ❑ making good eye contact?
  - ❑ facing the audience?

- How was my delivery? Did I:
  - ❑ have any verbal mannerisms that were distracting?
  - ❑ have any physical mannerisms that were distracting?
  - ❑ seem nervous or self-confident?
  - ❑ speak clearly and audibly?

- How were my visual aids? Were they:
  - ❑ clearly connected to my speech?
  - ❑ distracting or confusing?
  - ❑ easy to see?
  - ❑ too slow, too fast, or just right?

- How was the content of my speech? Did I:
  - ❑ clearly communicate my ideas?
  - ❑ provide examples and illustrations that made my points clear?
  - ❑ prove my opinion or clearly teach what I intended?
  - ❑ successfully persuade you or teach you something new?

- How well prepared am I? Do I need to:
  - ❑ strengthen my speech's content?
  - ❑ improve my visual aids?
  - ❑ remove distracting habits or mannerisms?
  - ❑ take some time for rest?

TIPS

- When using a video camera, do not have it handheld. Put it on a tripod, if possible.

- Ask your rehearsal audience to be cruel if necessary. Honest feedback is vital to improving your delivery.

- Practice with your visual aids, not without them. This will help you handle them effectively, and will also show you if they need to be improved.

- If at all possible, rehearse in the actual location of your speech. This will increase your confidence immensely while decreasing anxiety.

- Take some time off from your speech before the day arrives. A rested speaker is an effective speaker.

PRACTICE, PRACTICE, PRACTICE!

18 ▶ WHAT COMES NEXT?

The public have an insatiable curiosity to know everything. Except what is worth knowing.

—OSCAR WILDE, 1854–1900

LESSON SUMMARY

Your speech is actually not completed until you have answered your audience's questions. In this lesson, we will consider an effective question-and-answer session.

Well, you've done it—you've finally delivered your speech, and it's gone off without a hitch. You presented some stunning visual aids, made the audience laugh several times, made them stop and think seriously about your topic, and did it all with pizzazz. You conclude your thoughts with a compelling call to action, gather your notes, turn to leave the stage—and somebody raises a hand at the rear of the audience with a question. Uh oh. . . . You didn't rehearse for *that*!

The fact is, however, that no speech is concluded until the audience's questions are addressed. Yet, fielding questions is actually a good exercise for any speaker for a number of reasons. First, it forces the speaker to think through his or her material more fully, trying to anticipate what the audience might ask. Second, it gives the speaker some valuable practice with impromptu speaking, since there is no way you can script your answer to an unknown question.

Prepare in Advance

Okay, I just said you can't do this—but to some extent you can. That is, you don't know in advance what questions might be asked, but you can still make an educated guess. Ask yourself what questions *you* would ask if you heard someone give your speech, and then prepare to answer those questions.

When you rehearsed in front of your live audience, you asked them to hit you with some tough questions at the end of your speech (at least, you should have!). Use those sample questions as springboards to brainstorm what questions you might be asked when you give your speech, and then figure out what your answer would be.

Anticipating questions is a vital part of speechmaking. In fact, it's helpful to ask yourself from start to finish what questions you might have to face, since that can also help you to craft a more comprehensive speech. Knowing the questions in advance is like getting your hands on a final exam before it's given: You can spend time before the exam looking up the right answers, and then ace it when it's given! This might be called cheating when it comes to schoolwork, but when it comes to public speaking, it's called being prepared.

Control the Questions

You might think you have no control over what questions your audience asks, but that's not entirely true. You are the speaker, after all, which means that you are in charge, at least in some measure. You cannot control what the audience is thinking, but you can control the environment in which they ask questions.

For starters, reserve questions for the end of your speech. This is usually done by default, since most audiences understand this principle as basic etiquette. But you might have someone raise a hand while you're speaking, so don't be caught off guard. If that happens, pause and call upon the person with the question—it's possible that he or she simply can't hear you and wants you to speak louder. If the person asks a question about your topic, politely request that the audience hold their questions for the end, assuring that person that you will begin your question and answer time with him or her.

Sometimes you might be faced with a person who dominates the question time: The moment you answer one question, the person has another. You can control this situation as well simply by looking for others who have questions. Say, "That's another excellent question—I'll come back to it in a moment. But first, were there other questions?"

You can even control the atmosphere during the question time. Perhaps you've given a persuasive speech on a controversial topic, and some people in the audience hold strong opinions in a different direction. You might find yourself faced with a hostile attitude from someone in the audience, and you don't want to let that become the general atmosphere in the room.

You can defuse that hostility first and foremost by not returning it! Rephrase a question that is worded in an accusatory manner; thank an angry questioner for having the honesty to express those views; find a point of agreement, such as saying that you share the questioner's frustration on the topic and that you're both working toward the same goal of finding a solution. In short, you can control hostility by replying to it with respect and patience.

Follow Etiquette

This is actually an expansion on what we've just said about handling hostile questions: Treat everyone with courtesy. Your audience has treated you with courtesy by listening to your presentation and by holding questions to the end; now return the favor by following the basic rules of question-and-answer etiquette.

First, listen to the entire question. Do not interrupt the questioner when you think you've got the gist of the question; allow him or her to finish asking it. Frequently you'll find that the actual question was not what you'd anticipated because the questioner was trying to figure out exactly how to ask it. Once in a while, you might have an audience member who uses the question time to make a speech of his or her own—which is *not* following the practices of etiquette. Nevertheless, continue to be courteous; gently interrupt the questioner's impromptu speech by saying, "So I think the question you're asking is. . . ."

Another point of etiquette is to help questioners who get stuck for words. This is a far more common situation than hostility: An audience member has a question, but just can't seem to put it into satisfactory words. When the questioner begins to fumble for the right wording, help him or her out: "Yes, I think I understand what you're saying. In other words, why does. . . ." You will be rewarded with a warm smile of satisfaction when you reword the person's question and then answer it.

Etiquette also calls upon you as the speaker to make sure that everyone in the audience knows what question you're answering. This is definitely the most common situation you'll face in question times: A person stands and asks a question, directed at you, spoken in a conversational voice—and the rest of the audience didn't hear it. The solution is very simple: When the person is finished asking the question, restate what he or she said for the entire audience before answering it.

Treat each questioner like an intelligent adult. In fact, you should communicate a sense of genuine interest in the person's question. Do this by looking intently at the questioner, keeping your mind focused entirely upon the question. Don't just *look* like you're doing it; *do* it! It's entirely possible that the question will be something you addressed clearly and painstakingly in your speech; answer it as though you had inadvertently omitted that information. Remember times when you may have done the same thing, and avoid making that person feel embarrassed.

In short, treat your audience with respect and courtesy. Say "please" and "thank you"; make eye contact; listen intently; treat the questioner and the question with dignity.

Giving the Right Answer

When you prepared your speech, you did careful research; you took extensive notes; you organized your information carefully—and you did all these things for one reason: You wanted to be right! Wouldn't it be a tragedy then, if after all that work, you completely undercut your speech by giving wrong answers? Yet you will be amazed at how easily that can be done.

The very first rule in answering questions is this: *Don't guess!* If someone asks you something that you don't know, say so. It's really very simple, and there's no embarrassment or stigma attached at all. You were caught off guard, or the person asked about something beyond your expertise, and you don't know the answer. You have not lost credibility; in fact, you have gained it, because many people would be tempted to try thinking on their feet, inventing an answer as they go along, hoping that they hit the target by the end. They won't.

The next principle has been addressed in our previous section, but it bears repeating: Treat every question with dignity. This means you might be asked a question that seems so pathetically self-evident that you don't need to answer it. Answer it anyway, and do so as though you had omitted the answer in your speech, and you're grateful for the chance to correct that omission.

Keep your answers brief. Remember that you have a time limit, and that limit includes the time spent answering questions. If you spent your entire time on your speech, you're already going overtime while fielding questions—and this will definitely breed resentment in some of your audience. Be as succinct as you can when answering questions, and tell the audience that you can give them more information afterwards if they'd like it.

Do not introduce new material when answering questions. The question time should reinforce your speech, not give you an opportunity to make another one. If a complete answer requires new information, say so, offering to discuss it further afterwards. Your audience will appreciate your sensitivity to time, and those who are interested will appreciate your availability to inform them further.

Finally, correct any inaccuracies in a question. Being polite does not mean being coerced into saying something that you didn't mean. Perhaps a questioner misunderstood some portion of your speech: "When you said that blue is really yellow, what does that imply about green?" Of course, you didn't actually say that; the questioner misheard or misconstrued. So begin your answer by correcting the misconception, and then move on to answer the underlying question if one remains: "I think what I said was that blue and yellow are both primary colors—at least, that's what I'd intended to say. Green, of course, is a secondary color, so we can infer that..."

Notice that you don't accuse the questioner of deliberately misconstruing your speech. In fact, you offered to take some share of the blame in case you didn't clearly expound on what you'd intended to say. This defuses any potential hostility while still making it clear that you did not say what the questioner claims you said.

Invite the Audience to Answer

As a general rule, this approach is risky, because it implies that you are not a qualified expert on your topic. But it's far, far better than inventing an answer when you don't know it! Sometimes you will want to say, "I'm not sure of the answer to that question, but if you'll speak with me after I can arrange to get the information."

On the other hand, the question may involve some information that you are confident is known by others in the audience, at which point you can say, "I'm not sure, but I have no doubt that others here will know. Can anyone help us out on this?" This tactic, when used appropriately, shows the audience that you genuinely want to know more about your topic, and you are willing to admit that you don't know everything.

Opening and Closing the Question Time

Your speech conclusion is frequently not the conclusion of your speech; your speech concludes when all the audience's questions are answered (or as many as you have time to address). Nevertheless, your audience needs to have a clear sense that this is now the time when they can ask questions, and they also need to know when it's time to get up and leave.

Open your question time clearly: "And now I'd like to open the floor to anyone who has a question." This rewards the audience for observing etiquette by holding their questions to the end, and it primes the pump to get those questions flowing.

That said, however, you must be ready to face a few seconds of silence. Silence is like a death pall to a speechgiver; it's empty air waiting to be filled with the sound of your voice. But this is *not* the case when fielding questions, because the air needs to be filled by the audience, not by you. Allow approximately ten seconds of silence to give people a chance to formulate their questions.

If the silence continues toward half a minute, it's time for you to prime the pump yourself. You can get questions flowing by asking one: "Some of you may be wondering how my thoughts apply to the question of. . . ." Have this question planned before you begin speaking; that way it will be an intelligent question, *and* you'll know the answer! If you face silence after answering your own question, it means that you did an excellent job presenting your information. It's time to conclude.

"Well, if there are no questions, allow me to leave you with this thought." Notice that you have done two things: You have told the audience that the speech is over and it's time to leave; and you have summarized the gist of your speech. Your concluding thought, however, *must be brief*! You're putting your thoughts into a nutshell, encapsulating your entire speech in just one or two sentences. This gives your audience something to take home with them, and ends your speech on a strong note.

You will use this form of final conclusion whether you've had no questions or many. It brings the speech full circle, and ends with you in control as the expert on your topic. This may be an important tactic if you've been faced with challenging questions, as it will remind the audience that you are credible even if you don't know all the answers.

Exercise

Use this questionnaire yourself, and also give it to your practice audience before speaking, along with the questionnaire in Lesson 17:

- What questions did I raise in the audience's mind during my speech?

_____

_____

- What information was I sketchy on? What further information is needed?

_____

_____

- Did my examples illustrate my points? If not, what were the weak spots?

_____

_____

- Was I clear about my points and my conclusions? If not, where can I clarify?

_____

_____

- What were my presuppositions? How might my conclusions be different if my examples were different?

_____

_____

■ What were the weak spots in my reasoning? How might I be challenged by someone who disagrees with my conclusions?

_____

_____

_____

■ How do my conclusions relate to other topics, even unrelated ones?

_____

_____

_____

TIPS

- Always be courteous. Period.

- Defuse hostility by being courteous.

- Treat your questioners—and their questions—with dignity.

- Plan ahead by asking yourself what questions you might get. Give your rehearsal audience the questionnaires in this lesson and Lesson 17 to help you.

- Control the environment and the atmosphere during question times. Remember: You are in charge!

- Listen to the entire question before formulating an answer.

WHAT COMES NEXT?

19 ▶ COMMON SPEECH SITUATIONS

Eloquence is the essential thing in a speech, not information.

—MARK TWAIN, 1835–1910

LESSON SUMMARY

Most of what we've been covering in the previous lessons will apply in any speech situation. However, some situations require special considerations, as we'll see in this lesson.

I f you've paid attention to the quotations that open each lesson in this book, you might have noticed that Mark Twain appears frequently. Twain is best remembered as an author, most notably for *The Adventures of Tom Sawyer* and *The Adventures of Huckleberry Finn*. But you might not be aware that he was more famous in his own day as a public speaker and lecturer. In fact, Twain traveled extensively throughout the world on the lecture circuit, entertaining audiences around the globe with his wit and humor.

We tend to think of public speaking as a formal lecture given from on high before an audience that has gathered to listen. But the fact is that public speaking includes a wide variety of applications and settings, from answering a teacher's question in class to addressing the world via television. In this lesson, we'll address some of the more likely situations in which you'll be speaking publicly.

Making a Presentation

This is a very common occurrence, whether you are a student asked to present information to class, or a professional in the business world asked to provide a project update to your coworkers. You might be given some lead time for preparation, but you might just as likely find yourself called upon to speak on the spur of the moment.

Whether given advance notice or not, the goal is to *appear* as though you are well prepared. As we have said many times throughout these lessons, appearance is half the battle. If your audience believes you are confident in what you are saying, they will be far more likely to accept your message.

All the lessons in this book apply in this situation. If at all possible, you'll want to include visual aids to help get your ideas across. You'll want to make eye contact with your audience, and you'll want to be sure that your voice is clearly heard and understood. If you have time to prepare, you'll want to create an outline, and you'll want to expand your thoughts under several major sub-points, complete with explanations and illustrations of each.

The major asset you have in this situation is that you will probably know your audience quite well, whether they are fellow students or coworkers. This will enable you to assess how much they already know, helping you to focus on areas that will be new to them. You will also be able to gauge their reactions to your presentation, which is important in the office environment: Will they be pleased with your report, or will it produce resistance or disappointment? Knowing these things in advance will help you prepare for questions.

Public Meetings

I live in a small town, and I attend the town hall meetings frequently. My general purpose is simply to enjoy watching, taking advantage of something that is unique to America: the freedom to participate in the political process. But there are times when I need to participate more vocally, and I find myself speaking before an audience—actually, before two audiences: the town council, and the voters.

Such public forums bring with them a few distinguishing features worth mentioning. First, you may well find yourself addressing two or more different groups of listeners, each with radically different views on your topic. My town recently went through some fairly dramatic public meetings on zoning issues, and I found myself speaking to three distinct groups: the voters, most of whom vehemently opposed the development proposal; the "interested parties" and their lawyers (those directly involved in the proposed development); and the town council, allegedly neutral and impartial on the entire subject.

You will need to be sensitive to all the groups in your audience, knowing something of each group's views on the topic and how each will likely respond to your opinions. You will also quickly recognize from what you've learned in this book that public meetings will generally involve some sort of persuasive speech, so you should review Lesson 5 on how to create an effective persuasive argument.

Yet this also impinges on another unique feature of public meetings: severely limited time. You will probably not have the luxury of spending 40 minutes to expand and develop on your thesis; you will need to present a compelling argument in less than five minutes—and most local political settings will limit speakers to three minutes at the most. This leaves you with two options: present many points in little detail (our shotgun method), or present one point in greater detail (the rifle). Either can be effective, but generally the rifle is preferred, since other speakers will likely touch upon other arguments in detail. Just remember to use the courtroom analogy when planning your words: Provide your evidence, explain how it applies to your thesis, then summarize how your one major point proves your opinion to be the right one.

Other elements of public speaking come into play in this setting, as well. Eye contact, for example, is vitally important—although you may have to focus on one body and more or less ignore the rest of your audience. You will want to connect with those who make the decisions, since they are the ones whom you're trying to persuade. Nevertheless, you will want to speak clearly and be understood by everyone present, and you will *always* want to be courteous and polite. This last point can be a challenge at emotionally charged public gatherings, but your views will be far more attractive if you are polite.

Special Occasions

Weddings, funerals, birthdays, awards ceremonies, graduations, religious observances, extended family gatherings—they're all part of our lives, and sooner or later we all have to "share a few words" at one or another. You may know in advance that you'll be called upon to speak, or you might be asked spontaneously—but the end result is the same: Appear as though you are prepared, and appear as though you didn't prepare in advance.

You'll need to do this, of course, by preparing in advance! As we've said previously, the best way to approach such occasions is to think through what you'll want to say if asked, jotting some notes on an index card so you don't forget. Structure your thoughts to be suitable to the occasion and the time limit. Most special occasions will require some brief comments, limited perhaps to five minutes or less. This is probably not a time to expound in detail on some lengthy topic, nor is it an occasion for persuading your audience on some controversial issue. Keep your thoughts focused on the occasion, and keep them brief. Remember our fundamental rule for special occasions: The audience is there to honor the occasion, not to hear you speak.

Stressful Situations

Perhaps it's time for a raise, but your company has recently been laying off employees. Or perhaps you need to confront the directors of a civic organization concerning policies that have affected you. Maybe you need to make a class presentation that disagrees with the professor's viewpoints. Life is filled with stress and confrontation, but a skillful public speaker can easily carry the day.

Confrontation naturally breeds hostility, and the most important element of your presentation will be your demeanor. You will want to present a solid case, but you'll need to do it with humility and courtesy. If you come into the room with an arrogant air of self-righteousness, you'll lose your audience before you even begin.

For example, you might feel that your work responsibilities have grown far beyond your job description due to the recent layoffs. Don't approach your boss with an air of grievance or resentment; put yourself in his or her position and recognize that your boss has also been affected by the present crisis. Present your facts and requests, but also remember to acknowledge the difficulty of the situation, and do not place the blame on your audience. Create an atmosphere of team cooperation, and your boss will be more likely to join your side.

Finally, you will want to anticipate your audience's counterpoints. It is not enough simply to build a persuasive argument; you need to anticipate how your listeners will argue *against* your thesis. This follows the methods we considered in Lesson 18 on handling questions from the audience, except that in this situation your entire effectiveness will depend upon how well you address those questions. This form of public speaking actually comes closer to debate than to making a speech, and you will need to prepare yourself to present counterarguments to their counterarguments. If you can't answer any question or argument that might be thrown at you, you aren't ready to make your presentation.

Exercise

Use this questionnaire to outline your presentation:

1. What is the main purpose of this speech occasion? How does this purpose influence what I will say?

_____

_____

2. What is my time limit?

_____

_____

3. Who is my audience?

_____

_____

4. What is the occasion?
- ❑ Honorific (honoring someone; skip to question 9)
- ❑ Memorial (eulogizing someone; skip to question 9)
- ❑ Introductory (introducing someone; skip to question 9)
- ❑ Public meeting
- ❑ Confrontation
- ❑ Group presentation

5. If my audience will be several groups of opponents, which group will I focus on?

_____

_____

6. What is my thesis?

_____

_____

7. What aspect of my thesis will I expound in detail?

_____

_____

8. What illustrations and examples will I provide? (Skip questions 9–10.)

_____

_____

9. What story can I relate that is pertinent to the occasion?

_____

_____

10. What is the one thing I want my audience to remember about this occasion?

_____

_____

TIPS

- Appear confident, and your audience will respect your opinions.
- If you blame your audience for a problem, you will lose their cooperation.
- When faced with a divided audience, focus on those who need to be persuaded. This is most likely going to be the people who will make a final decision.
- Life is filled with stress and confrontation, but a skillful public speaker can easily carry the day.
- Present your arguments as though you and your audience are on the same team.

20 ▶ LEARNING FROM THE PROS

Imitation is the sincerest form of flattery.

—ANCIENT PROVERB

LESSON SUMMARY

The best way to learn a skill is to imitate the techniques of someone who has mastered that skill. This lesson presents some famous speeches, with questions on each to help you analyze what made them great.

Practice is the only way to learn any skill, as we've said many times already, but that practice should be coupled with imitation if you want to excel. If you want to become a great musician, you listen to great musicians and try to imitate their styles. Great painters learn by imitating the great masters; great writers hone their skill by imitating great writers.

Imitation is the inherent way that anyone learns anything. You learned how to speak by imitating your parents and siblings; you learned to walk by imitating those who walked. You can also learn to be a great speaker if you imitate those who have given great speeches.

In this lesson, we will examine some great speeches and see what we can learn from them. To help in this process, the background information will not be given for each speech (although it is provided at the end of this lesson), so that you can concentrate only on the words. Each speech will also provide exercise questions to help you analyze what made the speech great.

Speech 1

No man thinks more highly than I do of the patriotism, as well as abilities, of the very worthy gentlemen who have just addressed the House. But different men often see the same subject in different lights; and, therefore, I hope that it will not be thought disrespectful to those gentlemen, if, entertaining as I do opinions of a character very opposite to theirs, I shall speak forth my sentiments freely and without reserve.

This is no time for ceremony. The question before the House is one of awful moment to this country. For my own part, I consider it as nothing less than a question of freedom or slavery; and in proportion to the magnitude of the subject ought to be the freedom of the debate. It is only in this way that we can hope to arrive at truth, and fulfill the great responsibility which we hold to God and our country. Should I keep back my opinions at such a time, through fear of giving offense, I should consider myself as guilty of treason towards my country, and of an act of disloyalty towards the majesty of heaven, which I revere above all earthly kings.

Mr. President, it is natural to man to indulge in the illusions of hope. We are apt to shut our eyes against a painful truth, and listen to the song of that siren, till she transforms us into beasts. Is this the part of wise men, engaged in a great and arduous struggle for liberty? Are we disposed to be of the number of those who, having eyes, see not, and having ears, hear not, the things which so nearly concern their temporal salvation?

For my part, whatever anguish of spirit it may cost, I am willing to know the whole truth—to know the worst and to provide for it. I have but one lamp by which my feet are guided; and that is the lamp of experience. I know of no way of judging of the future but by the past. And judging by the past, I wish to know what there has been in the conduct of the British ministry for the last ten years, to justify those hopes with which gentlemen have been pleased to solace themselves and the House?

Is it that insidious smile with which our petition has been lately received? Trust it not, sir; it will prove a snare to your feet. Suffer not yourselves to be betrayed with a kiss. Ask yourselves how this gracious reception of our petition comports with these warlike preparations which cover our waters and darken our land. Are fleets and armies necessary to a work of love and reconciliation? Have we shown ourselves so unwilling to be reconciled that force must be called in to win back our love? Let us not deceive ourselves, sir. These are the implements of war and subjugation—the last arguments to which kings resort. I ask gentlemen, sir, what means this martial array, if its purpose be not to force us to submission? Can gentlemen assign any other possible motives for it? Has Great Britain any enemy, in this quarter of the world, to call for all this accumulation of navies and armies?

No, sir, she has none. They are meant for us; they can be meant for no other. They are sent over to bind and rivet upon us those chains which the British ministry have been so long forging. And what have we to oppose to them? Shall we try argument? Sir, we have been trying that for the last ten years. Have we anything new to offer on the subject? Nothing.

We have held the subject up in every light of which it is capable; but it has been all in vain. Shall we resort to entreaty and humble supplication? What terms shall we find which have not been already exhausted? Let us not, I beseech you, sir, deceive ourselves longer.

Sir, we have done everything that could be done to avert the storm which is now coming on. We have petitioned; we have remonstrated; we have supplicated; we have prostrated ourselves before the throne, and have implored its interposition to arrest the tyrannical hands of the ministry and Parliament.

Our petitions have been slighted; our remonstrances have produced additional violence and insult; our supplications have been disregarded; and we have been spurned, with contempt, from the foot of the throne. In vain, after these things, may we indulge the fond hope of peace and reconciliation. There is no longer any room for hope.

If we wish to be free—if we mean to preserve inviolate those inestimable privileges for which we have been so long contending—if we mean not basely to abandon the noble struggle in which we have been so long engaged, and which we have pledged ourselves never to abandon until the glorious object of our contest shall be obtained, we must fight! I repeat it, sir, we must fight! An appeal to arms and to the God of Hosts is all that is left us!

They tell us, sir, that we are weak—unable to cope with so formidable an adversary. But when shall we be stronger? Will it be the next week, or the next year? Will it be when we are totally disarmed, and when a British guard shall be stationed in every house? Shall we gather strength by irresolution and inaction? Shall we acquire the means of effectual resistance, by lying supinely on our backs, and hugging the delusive phantom of hope, until our enemies shall have bound us hand and foot?

Sir, we are not weak, if we make a proper use of the means which the God of nature hath placed in our power. Three millions of people, armed in the holy cause of liberty, and in such a country as that which we possess, are invincible by any force which our enemy can send against us. Besides, sir, we shall not fight our battles alone. There is a just God who presides over the destinies of nations, and who will raise up friends to fight our battles for us.

The battle, sir, is not to the strong alone; it is to the vigilant, the active, the brave. Besides, sir, we have no election. If we were base enough to desire it, it is now too late to retire from the contest. There is no retreat but in submission and slavery! Our chains are forged! Their clanking may be heard on the plains of Boston! The war is inevitable—and let it come! I repeat it, sir, let it come!

It is in vain, sir, to extenuate the matter. Gentlemen may cry, "Peace! Peace!"—but there is no peace. The war is actually begun! The next gale that sweeps from the north will bring to our ears the clash of resounding arms! Our brethren are already in the field! Why stand we here idle? What is it that gentlemen wish? What would they have? Is life so dear, or peace so sweet, as to be purchased at the price of chains and slavery? Forbid it, Almighty God! I know not what course others may take; but as for me, give me liberty, or give me death!

Exercise

■ What is the speaker's thesis?

_____

_____

■ What objections does the speaker anticipate? How does he counter those suggestions in his speech?

_____

_____

■ What problems does the speaker address? What solutions does he offer?

_____

_____

■ What is the speaker's call to action for his audience?

_____

_____

Speech 2

Fans, for the past two weeks you have been reading about a bad break I got. Yet today I consider myself the luckiest man on the face of the earth. I have been in ballparks for seventeen years and have never received anything but kindness and encouragement from you fans.

Look at these grand men. Which of you wouldn't consider it the highlight of his career to associate with them for even one day?

Sure, I'm lucky. Who wouldn't consider it an honor to have known Jacob Ruppert—also the builder of baseball's greatest empire, Ed Barrow—to have spent the next nine years with that wonderful little fellow Miller Huggins—then to have spent the next nine years with that outstanding leader, that smart student of psychology, the best manager in baseball today, Joe McCarthy!

Sure, I'm lucky. When the New York Giants, a team you would give your right arm to beat, and vice versa, sends you a gift, that's something! When everybody down to the groundskeepers and those boys in white coats remember you with trophies, that's something.

When you have a wonderful mother-in-law who takes sides with you in squabbles against her own daughter, that's something. When you have a father and mother who work all their lives so that you can have an education and build your body, it's a blessing! When you have a wife who has been a tower of strength and shown more courage than you dreamed existed, that's the finest I know.

So I close in saying that I might have had a tough break—but I have an awful lot to live for!

Exercise

■ What is the probable occasion of this speech?

_____

_____

■ In what ways is the speaker's tone and delivery appropriate to that occasion? How does this speech differ from a persuasive speech?

_____

_____

■ This was a somewhat sad occasion. Why did the speaker keep repeating that he was lucky? Why is this an effective technique for sad occasions?

_____

_____

Speech 3

Four score and seven years ago our fathers brought forth on this continent, a new nation, conceived in liberty, and dedicated to the proposition that all men are created equal.

Now we are engaged in a great civil war, testing whether that nation, or any nation so conceived and so dedicated, can long endure. We are met on a great battlefield of that war. We have come to dedicate a portion of that field, as a final resting place for those who here gave their lives that that nation might live. It is altogether fitting and proper that we should do this.

But in a larger sense, we cannot dedicate—we cannot consecrate—we cannot hallow—this ground. The brave men, living and dead, who struggled here, have consecrated it, far above our poor power to add or detract. The world will little note, nor long remember, what we say here, but it can never forget what they did here. It is for us the living, rather, to be dedicated here to the unfinished work which they who fought here have thus far so nobly advanced. It is rather for us to be here dedicated to the great task remaining before us—that from these honored dead we take increased devotion to that cause for which they gave the last full measure of devotion—that we here highly resolved that these dead shall not have died in vain—that this nation, under God, shall have a new birth of freedom—and that government of the people, by the people, for the people, shall not perish from the earth.

Exercise

■ What is the occasion of this speech? Who is likely in the audience?

_____

_____

■ Why does the speaker say that "The world will little note, nor long remember, what we say here"? How does this approach focus attention on the occasion rather than the speech?

_____

_____

■ Why does the speaker begin by saying, "Four score and seven years ago," rather than saying, "Eighty-seven years ago"? How does this wording help the speech?

_____

_____

■ How does the speaker use this somber occasion to call the audience to action? Why is it appropriate here?

_____

_____

Speech 4

Mr. Vice President, Mr. Speaker, members of the Senate and the House of Representatives:

Yesterday, December 7, 1941—a date which will live in infamy—the United States of America was suddenly and deliberately attacked by naval and air forces of the Empire of Japan.

The United States was at peace with that nation, and, at the solicitation of Japan, was still in conversation with its government and its Emperor looking toward the maintenance of peace in the Pacific.

Indeed, one hour after Japanese air squadrons had commenced bombing in the American island of Oahu, the Japanese Ambassador to the United States and his colleague delivered to our Secretary of State a formal reply to a recent American message. And, while this reply stated that it seemed useless to continue the existing diplomatic negotiations, it contained no threat or hint of war or of armed attack.

It will be recorded that the distance of Hawaii from Japan makes it obvious that the attack was deliberately planned many days or even weeks ago. During the intervening time the Japanese Government has deliberately sought to deceive the United States by false statements and expressions of hope for continued peace.

The attack yesterday on the Hawaiian Islands has caused severe damage to American naval and military forces. I regret to tell you that very many American lives have been lost. In addition, American ships have been reported torpedoed on the high seas between San Francisco and Honolulu.

Yesterday the Japanese Government also launched an attack against Malaya. Last night Japanese forces attacked Hong Kong. Last night Japanese forces attacked Guam. Last night Japanese forces attacked the Philippine Islands. Last night the Japanese attacked Wake Island. And this morning the Japanese attacked Midway Island.

Japan has therefore undertaken a surprise offensive extending throughout the Pacific area. The facts of yesterday and today speak for themselves. The people of the United States have already formed their opinions and well understand the implications to the very life and safety of our nation.

As Commander-in-Chief of the Army and Navy I have directed that all measures be taken for our defense, that always will our whole nation remember the character of the onslaught against us.

No matter how long it may take us to overcome this premeditated invasion, the American people, in their righteous might, will win through to absolute victory.

I believe that I interpret the will of the Congress and of the people when I assert that we will not only defend ourselves to the uttermost but will make it very certain that this form of treachery shall never again endanger us.

Hostilities exist. There is no blinking at the fact that our people, our territory, and our interests are in grave danger.

With confidence in our armed forces, with the unbounding determination of our people, we will gain the inevitable triumph. So help us God.

I ask that the Congress declare that since the unprovoked and dastardly attack by Japan on Sunday, December 7, 1941, a state of war has existed between the United States and the Japanese Empire.

Exercise

- What does the speaker mean by "a date which will live in infamy"? How is that better than merely saying "a sad day, indeed"?

_____

_____

- Why does the speaker spend time explaining that Japan had deliberately deceived the United States? What objections was he anticipating to his speech? How did this counter those anticipated objections?

_____

_____

- What call to action does the speaker make of his audience? How has he strengthened his argument in order to urge his audience to take that action?

_____

_____

- How has the speaker taken a stressful speech situation and turned it to his advantage?

_____

_____

Who Said It?

Speech 1: Patrick Henry, March 23, 1775. Henry was addressing the political leaders of Virginia at a time when the state was still a colony of Great Britain. His speech helped to motivate Virginia to join forces with the colonies of New England, leading to the American Revolution.

Speech 2: Lou Gehrig, July 4, 1939. Gehrig was the first baseman for the New York Yankees, one of the greats of baseball history. His career was cut short, however, when he contracted a spinal disease which today is known as Lou Gehrig's Disease. He gave this speech as his farewell to baseball, and died two years later.

Speech 3: Abraham Lincoln, November 19, 1863. Lincoln was speaking at Gettysburg, Pennsylvania, the site of a horrific battle during the American Civil War. His purpose was to dedicate a cemetery at that site, but his words still ring through history today. His speech lasted approximately two minutes.

Speech 4: Franklin D. Roosevelt, December 8, 1941. President Roosevelt gave this speech the day after the Japanese bombed Pearl Harbor. His words led the United States into war against Japan, Germany, and Italy—World War II.

APPENDIX

SUMMARY

The following appendix provides a brief grammar overview. Knowledge of basic grammar is an important part of being able to express your ideas clearly. This should be a helpful reference as you prepare your speech.

Sentence structure refers to the way we compose sentences: how we string subjects, verbs, objects, and modifiers together in clauses and phrases. Awkward or incorrect placement of phrases and clauses can result in sentences that are confusing or unclear, or say things that you don't mean. Sentence structure is also important to style. If sentence structure is too simple or repetitive, the writing becomes monotonous for the reader.

Subjects, Predicates, and Objects

When we write, we express our ideas in sentences. But what is a sentence, anyway?

The **sentence** is our basic unit of written expression. It consists of two essential parts—a **subject** and a **predicate**—and it must express a complete thought. The subject of a sentence tells us *who* or *what* the sentence is about—who or what is performing the action of the sentence. The predicate tells us something *about* the subject—what the subject is or does. Thus, in the following sentence:

The phone is ringing.

The word *phone* is the subject. It tells us what the sentence is about—who or what performs the action of the sentence. The verb phrase *is ringing* is the predicate. It tells us the action performed by (or information about) the subject.

The subject of a sentence can be **singular** or **compound** (plural):

I slept all day.	*Kendrick and I worked all night.*
singular subject	compound subject (two subjects performing the action)

The predicate can also be singular or compound:

I bought a present.	*I bought a present and wrapped it beautifully.*
singular predicate	compound predicate (two actions performed by the subject)

In many sentences, someone or something "receives" the action expressed in the predicate. This person or thing is called the **direct object**. In the following sentences, the subject and predicate are separated by a slash (/) and the direct object is underlined:

I / bought a present. (The present receives the action of being bought.)
Jane / loves ice cream. (Ice cream receives the action of being loved by Jane.)

Sentences can also have an **indirect object**: a person or thing who "receives" the direct object. In the following sentences, the direct object is underlined and the indirect object is in bold:

I / gave **Sunil** *a present.* (Sunil receives the present; the present receives the action of being given.)
The reporter / asked **the president** *a question.* (The president receives the question; the question receives the action of being asked.)

Independent and Dependent Clauses

A **clause** contains a subject and a predicate and may also have direct and indirect objects. An **independent clause** expresses a complete thought; it can stand on its own as a sentence. A **dependent clause**, on the other hand, cannot stand alone because it expresses an incomplete idea. When a dependent clause stands alone, the result is a **sentence fragment**.

Independent clause: *She was excited.*
Dependent clause: *Because she was excited.*

Notice that the dependent clause is incomplete; it needs an additional thought to make a complete sentence, such as:

She spoke very quickly because she was excited.

The independent clause, however, can stand alone. It is a complete thought.

Subordinating Conjunctions

What makes a dependent clause dependent is a **subordinating conjunction** such as the word *because*. Subordinating conjunctions connect clauses and help show the relationship between those clauses. Here is a list of the most common subordinating conjunctions:

after	even though	that	when
although	if	though	where
as, as if	in order that	unless	wherever
because	once	until	while
before	since		

When a clause begins with a subordinating conjunction, it is dependent. It must be connected to an independent clause to become a complete thought:

I never knew true happiness   *until I met you.*
independent clause   dependent clause

After Johnson quit,   *I had to work overtime.*
dependent clause   independent clause

A sentence with both a dependent clause (DC) and independent clause (IC) is called a **complex sentence**. Both of the previous sentences are complex sentences.

Conjunctive Adverbs

A very common grammar mistake is to think that words such as *however* and *therefore* are subordinating conjunctions. *However* and *therefore* belong to a group of words called **conjunctive adverbs**. These words also signal relationships between parts of a sentence. When they are used with a semicolon, they can combine independent clauses.

also	indeed	now
anyway	instead	otherwise
besides	likewise	similarly
certainly	meanwhile	still
finally	moreover	then
furthermore	namely	therefore
however	nevertheless	thus
incidentally	next	undoubtedly

PART OF SPEECH	FUNCTION	EXAMPLES
noun	names a person, place, thing, or concept	*water, Byron, telephone, Main Street, tub, virtue*
pronoun	takes the place of a noun so that the noun does not have to be repeated	*I, you, he, she, us, they, this, that, themselves, somebody, who, which*
verb	describes an action, occurrence, or state of being	*wait, seem, be, visit, renew*
helping verb (also called auxillary verb)	combines with other verbs (main verbs) to create verb phrases that help indicate tenses	forms, of *be, do,* and *have; can, could, might, must, shall, should, will, would*
adjective	describes nouns and pronouns; can also identify or quantify	*green, round, old, surprising; that* (e.g., *that elephant*); *several* (e.g., *several elephants*)
adverb	describes verbs, adjectives, other adverbs, or entire clauses	*dreamily, quickly, always, very, then*
preposition	expresses the relationship in time or space between words in a sentence	*in, on, around, above, between, underneath, beside, with, upon* (see the following list)

PREPOSITIONS: A SHORT LIST

Prepositions are extremely important: They help us understand how objects relate to each other in space and time. Recognizing them can help you quickly check for subject-verb agreement and other grammar issues. Here is a list of the most common prepositions. See the section on usage for notes about the most common prepositional idioms.

about	at	besides	except	like	outside	to	with
above	before	between	for	near	over	toward	without
across	behind	beyond	from	of	since	under	
after	below	by	in	off	through	until	
against	beneath	down	inside	on	throughout	up	
around	beside	during	into	out	till	upon	

Here are some examples:

I didn't go to the party; <u>instead</u>, I stayed home and watched a good film.

Samantha is a fabulous cook; <u>indeed</u>, she may even be better than Jacque.

I need to pay this bill immediately. <u>Otherwise</u>, my phone service will be cut off.

I am tall, and he is short.
[IC, coordinating conjunction + IC]

I am tall; he is short.
[IC; IC]

I was late, yet I still got the account.
[IC, coordinating conjunction + IC]

Compound Sentences and Coordinating Conjunctions

When two independent clauses are combined, the result is a **compound sentence** like the following:

He was late, so he lost the account.

The most common way to join two independent clauses is with a comma and a coordinating conjunction: *and, but, or, nor, for, so, yet.* Independent clauses can also be joined with a semicolon if the ideas in the sentences are closely related.

Sentence Boundaries

Expressing complete ideas and clearly indicating where sentences begin and end are essential to effective writing. Two of the most common grammatical errors with sentence boundaries are fragments and run-ons.

Incomplete Sentences (Fragments)

As we stated earlier, a complete sentence must (1) have both a **subject** (who or what performs the action) and a **verb** (a state of being or an action), and (2) express a complete thought. If you don't complete a thought, or if you are missing a subject or verb (or both), then you have an **incomplete sentence** (also called a sentence

fragment). To correct a fragment, add the missing subject or verb or otherwise change the sentence to complete the thought.

Incomplete:	Which is simply not true. [No subject. (*Which* is not a subject.)]
Complete:	*That* is simply not true.
Incomplete:	For example, the French Revolution. [No verb.]
Complete:	*The best example is* the French Revolution.
Incomplete:	Even though the polar icecaps are melting. [Subject and verb, but not a complete thought.]
Complete:	<u>Some people still don't believe in global warming</u> even though the polar icecaps are melting.

Run-On Sentences

A **run-on** sentence occurs when one sentence "runs" right into the next without proper punctuation between them. Usually, there's either no punctuation at all or just a comma between the two thoughts. But commas alone are not strong enough to separate two complete ideas. Here are some examples of run-ons:

> *Let's go it's getting late.*
> *Whether or not you believe me it's true, I didn't lie to you.*

There are five ways to correct run-on sentences:

1. With a period
2. With a comma and a coordinating conjunction: *and, or, nor, for, so, but, yet*
3. With a semicolon
4. With a dash

5. With a subordinating conjunction to create a dependent clause: *although, because, during, while,* etc.

Here's a run-on sentence corrected with each of these techniques:

Run-on:	The debate is over, now it is time to vote.
Period:	The debate is over. Now it is time to vote.
Comma + conjunction:	The debate is over, and now it is time to vote.
Semicolon:	The debate is over; now it is time to vote.
Dash:	The debate is over—now it is time to vote.
Subordinating conjunction:	Since the debate is over, it is time to vote.

Parts of Speech: A Brief Review

A word's *function* and *form* is determined by its **part of speech**. The word *calm*, for example, can be either a verb (*calm* down) or an adjective (a *calm* afternoon); it changes to *calmly* when it is an adverb (they discussed the matter *calmly*). Be sure you know the different parts of speech and the job each part of speech performs in a sentence.

Phrases and Modifiers

Sentences are often "filled out" by **phrases** and **modifiers**. Phrases are groups of words that *do not* have both a subject and predicate; they might have either a subject or a verb, but not both, and sometimes neither. Modifiers are words and phrases that qualify or describe people, places, things, and actions. The most common phrases are **prepositional phrases**, which consist of a preposition and a noun or pronoun (e.g., *in the attic*). Modifiers include **adjectives** (e.g., *slow, blue, excellent*) and **adverbs** (e.g., *cheerfully, suspiciously*). In the following examples, the prepositional phrases are underlined and the modifiers are in bold:

> He was **very** late <u>for an important</u> meeting <u>with a new</u> client.

> He **brazenly** took her wallet <u>from her purse</u> when she got up <u>from the table</u> to go <u>to the **ladies'** room.</u>

Placement of Modifiers

As a general rule, words, phrases, or clauses that describe nouns and pronouns should be as close as possible to the words they describe. *The relaxing music,* for example, is better (clearer, more concise and precise) than *the music that is relaxing.* In the first sentence, the modifier *relaxing* is right next to the word it modifies (*music*).

When modifiers are not next to the words they describe, you not only often use extra words, but you might also end up with a **misplaced** or **dangling modifier** and a sentence that means something other than what was intended. This is especially true of phrases and clauses that work as modifiers. Take a look at the following sentence, for example:

> Racing to the car, I watched him trip and drop his bag.

Who was racing to the car? Because the modifier *racing to the car* is next to *I,* the sentence says that *I* was doing the racing. But the verb *watched* indicates that *he* was the one racing to the car. Here are two corrected versions:

> I watched as he raced to the car and dropped his bag.

> I watched as, racing to the car, he dropped his bag.

In the first sentence, the phrase *racing to the car* has been revised to *raced to the car* and given the appropriate subject, *he.* In the second sentence, *racing to the car* is right next to the modified element (*he*).

Here's another example:

> Growling ferociously, I watched as the lions approached each other.

It's quite obvious that it was the lions, not the speaker, that were growling ferociously. But because the modifier (*growling ferociously*) isn't right next to what it modifies (*the lions*), the sentence actually says that *I* was growling ferociously. Here's the corrected version:

> I watched as the lions, growling ferociously, approached each other.

Again, the sentence is clearer now because the modifier is right next to what it modifies.

Sometimes these errors can be corrected simply by moving the modifier to the right place (next to what it modifies). Other times, you may need to add a subject and verb to clarify who or what is modified by the phrase. Here are some more examples of misplaced and dangling modifiers and their corrections:

<u>Incorrect:</u> *Worn and tattered, Uncle Joe took down the flag.*

<u>Correct:</u> *Uncle Joe took down the flag, which was worn and tattered.* OR *Uncle Joe took down the worn, tattered flag.*

Incorrect: *While making breakfast, the smoke alarm went off and woke the baby.*

Correct: *While I was making breakfast, the smoke alarm went off and woke the baby.* OR
The smoke alarm went off and woke the baby while I was making breakfast.

Parallel Structure

Parallel structure is an important part of effective writing. It means that words and phrases in the sentence follow the same grammatical pattern. This makes ideas easier to follow and expresses ideas more gracefully. Notice how parallelism works in the following examples:

Not parallel: *We came, we saw, and it was conquered by us.*
(The first two clauses use the active *we + past tense verb* construction; the third uses a passive structure with a prepositional phrase.)

Parallel: *We came, we saw, we conquered.*
(All three clauses start with *we* and use a past tense verb.)

Not parallel: *Please be sure to throw out your trash, place your silverware in the bin, and your tray should go on the counter.*
(Two verbs follow the *to + verb + your + noun* pattern; the third puts the noun first, then the verb.)

Parallel: *Please be sure to throw out your trash, place your silverware in the bin, and put your tray on the counter.*
(All three items follow the *to + verb + your + noun* [+ *prepositional phrase*] pattern.)

Parallelism is most often needed in lists, as in the previous examples, and in the *not only/but also* sentence pattern.

Hermione's nervousness was exacerbated not only by the large crowd, but also by the bright lights.
(Each phrase has a preposition, an adjective, and a noun.)

Their idea was not only the most original; it was also the most practical.
(Each phrase uses the superlative form of an adjective—see the Appendix section on usage for more information on superlatives.)

Active and Passive Voice

In most cases, effective writing will use the **active voice** as much as possible. In an active sentence, the subject performs the action:

James filed the papers yesterday.
Jin Lee sang the song beautifully.

In a **passive** sentence, on the other hand, the subject is passive. Rather than performing the action, the subject is *acted upon*:

The papers were filed by James yesterday.
The song was sung beautifully by Jin Lee.

Active sentences are more direct, powerful, and clear. They often use fewer words and have less room for confusion. There are times when the passive voice is preferred, such as when the source of the action is not known or when the writer wants to emphasize the recipient of the action rather than the performer of the action:

Protective gear must be worn by everyone entering this building.

As a general rule, however, sentences should be active whenever possible.

Usage

Usage refers to the rules that govern the form of the words we use and how we string those words together in sentences. Correct grammar and usage are essential for clear and effective communication. In this section, you will review the following areas of basic grammar and usage:

1. Verb conjugation and usage
2. Consistent verb tense
3. Subject-verb agreement
4. Gerunds and infinitives
5. Pronoun cases
6. Pronoun agreement
7. Comparative and superlative adjectives and adverbs
8. Prepositional idioms

Verbs

Verbs are the "heart" of a sentence. They express the action or *state of being* of the subject, telling us what the subject is doing, thinking, or feeling.

> She **yelled** out the window. (action)
> I **am** happy to be here. (state of being)
> We **feel** very lucky **to be** alive. (state of being)
> I **should ask** Winston what he **thinks**. (action)

Verbs have five basic forms:

1. **Infinitive:** the base form of the verb plus the word *to*.

   > *to go   to be   to dream   to admire*

   To indicate tenses of regular verbs (when the action of the verb did occur, is occurring, or will occur), we use the base form of the verb and add the appropriate tense endings.

2. **Present tense:** the verb form that expresses what is happening now.

   > I **am** sorry you **are** not coming with us.

   > Jessica **does** yoga every morning.

   The present tense of regular verbs is formed as follows:

	SINGULAR	PLURAL
first person (*I/we*)	base form (*believe*)	base form (*believe*)
second person (*you*)	base form (*believe*)	base form (*believe*)
third person (*he/she/it/they*)	base form + -s/-es (*believes*)	base form (*believe*)

3. **Present participle:** the verb form that describes what is happening now. It ends in *-ing* and is accompanied by a helping verb such as *is*.

   > Jessica *is doing* a difficult yoga pose.

   > The leaves *are falling* from the trees.

   Note: Words that end in *-ing* don't always function as verbs. Sometimes they act as nouns and are called **gerunds**. They can also function as adjectives (called **participial phrases**).

   Present participle
   (verb):   He *is loading* the boxes into the car.

   Gerund
   (noun):   This parking area is for *loading* only.

   Participial phrase
   (adjective):   The *loading* dock is littered with paper.

   (You will learn more about gerunds later in this section.)

PRESENT	PAST PARTICIPLE	PAST	PAST PARTICIPLE
ask	asking	asked	asked
dream	dreaming	dreamed	dreamed
protect	protecting	protected	protected
spell	spelling	spelled	spelled
whistle	whistling	whistled	whistled

4. **Past tense:** the verb form that expresses what happened in the past.

> It <u>snowed</u> yesterday in the mountains.

> I <u>felt</u> better after I <u>stretched</u> and <u>did</u> some deep breathing.

5. **Past participle:** the verb form that describes an action that happened in the past and is used with a helping verb, such as *has, have,* or *had.*

> It <u>has</u> not <u>snowed</u> all winter.

> I <u>have waited</u> as long as I can.

Regular Verbs

Most English verbs are "regular"—they follow a standard set of rules for forming the present participle, past tense, and past participle.

- The present participle is formed by adding -*ing.*
- The past and past participle are formed by adding -*ed.*
- If the verb ends with the letter *e,* just add *d.*
- If the verb ends with the letter *y,* for the past tense, change the *y* to an *i* and add -*ed.*

A handful of English verbs have the same present, past, and past participle form. Here is a partial list of those verbs and several examples:

SAME PRESENT, PAST, AND PAST PARTICIPLE FORM

bet	hit	set
bid	hurt	shut
burst	put	spread
cost	quit	upset
cut	read	

<u>Present:</u>   I **read** the newspaper every morning.

<u>Past:</u>   I **read** the newspaper yesterday morning.

<u>Past participle:</u>   I **have read** the newspaper every morning since 1992.

Irregular Verbs

About 150 English verbs are **irregular.** They don't follow the standard rules for changing tense. We can divide these irregular verbs into three categories:

1. irregular verbs with the same *past* and *past participle* forms
2. irregular verbs with three distinct forms
3. irregular verbs with the same *present* and *past participle* forms

The following table lists a few examples of irregular verbs.

PRESENT	PAST	PAST PARTICIPLE
Same past and past participle forms:		
bite	bit	bit
dig	dug	dug
hear	heard	heard
leave	left	left
Three distinct forms:		
begin	began	begun
ring	rang	rung
sing	sang	sung
spring	sprang	sprung
Same present and past participle forms:		
come	came	come
overcome	overcame	overcome
run	ran	run

In English, as in many other languages, the essential verb *to be* is highly irregular:

SUBJECT	PRESENT	PAST	PAST PARTICIPLE
I	am	was	have been
you	are	were	have been
he, she, it	is	was	has been
we	are	were	have been
they	are	were	have been

Helping Verbs

Helping verbs (also called **auxiliary verbs**) are essential to clear communication. They help indicate exactly when an action took place or will take place. They also suggest very specific meanings, such as the subject's ability or intention to do something. The following table lists the helping verbs, their forms, and their meanings.

PRESENT & FUTURE	PAST	MEANING	EXAMPLES
will, shall	would	intention	*She will meet us at the hotel.* *They said they would call first.*
can	could	ability	*I can be there in ten minutes.* *Rose could find only one glove.*
may, might, can, could	could, might	permission	*May I tag along?* *Could we get together after the meeting?*
should	should + have + past participle	recommendation	*We should leave before the snow starts.* *They should have known better.*
must, have (to)	had (to)	necessity	*I must go to the dentist.* *I had to have two teeth pulled.*
should	should + have + past participle	expectation	*They should be on the next train.* *They should have been on that train.*
may, might	might + have + past participle	possibility	*They may be lost.* *They might have gotten lost.*

Subjunctive Mood

The **subjunctive mood** is one of the verb forms we often forget to use in conversation, and therefore we often neglect to use it correctly in our writing. Like helping verbs, the subjunctive is used to express a specific meaning, indicating something that is wished for or that is contrary to fact. It is formed by using *were* instead of *was* as in the following examples:

> *If she <u>were</u> a little more experienced, she would get the promotion.* (She is not a little more experienced.)

> *If I <u>were</u> rich, I would travel the world.* (Unfortunately, I am not rich.)

Troublesome Verbs

Three verb pairs are particularly troublesome, even for native speakers of English:

> *lie / lay*
> *sit / set*
> *rise / raise*

The key to knowing which verb to use is remembering which verb takes an object. In each pair, one verb is **transitive**—an object "receives" the action—while the other is **intransitive**—the subject itself "receives" or performs the action. For example, *lie* is an action that the subject of the sentence "performs" on itself: *I will <u>lie</u> down.* The transitive verb *lay*, on the other hand, is an action that the subject of the sentence performs upon an object: *I lay the baby down in the crib.* In the following examples, the subjects are in bold and the objects are underlined.

lie: to rest or recline (intransitive—subject only)
lay: to put or place (transitive—needs an object)

> *I will lie down for a while.*
> *Will **you** please lay the papers down on the table?*

sit: to rest (intransitive—subject only)
set: to put or place (transitive—needs an object)

*Why don't **we** sit down and talk this over?*
He will set the record straight.

rise: to go up (intransitive—subject only)
raise: to move something up (transitive—needs an object)

> *The **sun** will rise at 5:48 A.M. tomorrow.*
> *He raised the rent to $750 per month.*

The basic forms of these verbs can also be a bit tricky. The following table shows how each verb is conjugated.

PRESENT	PRESENT PARTICIPLE (WITH *AM, IS, ARE*)	PAST	PAST PARTICIPLE (WITH *HAVE, HAS, HAD*)
lie, lies	lying	lay	lain
lay, lays	laying	laid	laid
sit, sits	sitting	sat	sat
sets, sets	setting	set	set
rise, rises	rising	rose	risen
raise, raises	raising	raised	raised

Now that you have reviewed verb conjugation and tense formation, it's time to talk about two key issues with verb usage: consistent tense and subject-verb agreement.

Consistent Tense

One of the quickest ways to confuse people, especially if you are telling a story or describing an event, is to shift verb tenses. To help listeners be clear about *when* actions occur, make sure verbs are consistent in tense. If you begin telling the story in the present tense, for example, keep the story in the present tense; do not inadvertently mix tenses. Be clear about changing tense, and make sure that it makes sense in the context of the story (for example, a story that takes place in the present tense might use the past tense to talk about actions that happened before the story started). Otherwise, you will leave your audience wondering whether actions are taking place in the present or took place in the past.

Incorrect: *She left the house and forgets her keys again.*

Correct: *She left the house and forgot her keys again.*

Incorrect: *When we work together, we got better results.*

Correct: *When we work together, we get better results.* OR
When we worked together, we got better results.

Agreement

In English grammar, **agreement** means that sentence elements are balanced. Verbs, for example, should *agree* with their subjects: If the subject is singular, the verb should be singular; if the subject is plural, the verb should be plural.

> Incorrect: *They doesn't have a chance against Coolidge.*
> (plural subject, singular verb)
>
> Correct: *They don't have a chance against Coolidge.*
> (plural subject, plural verb)

Of course, to make sure subjects and verbs agree, you need to be clear about who or what is the subject of the sentence. For example, what is the subject in the following sentence, and which is the correct verb?

> *Only one of the students [was/were] officially registered for the class.*

In this sentence, the subject is *one*, not *students*. Though it seems like *students* are performing the action of being completed, *students* can't be the subject because it is part of a prepositional phrase (*of the students*), and **subjects are never found in prepositional phrases**. Thus, the verb must be singular (*was*, not *were*) to agree with *one*. In addition, it is only **one** of the students—not all—who was registered, so again, the verb must be singular.

Here are some other important guidelines for subject-verb agreement:

- If a compound, singular subject is connected by *and*, the verb must be plural.

  Both <u>Vanessa and Xui want</u> to join the committee.

- If a compound, singular subject is connected by *or* or *nor*, the verb must be singular.

  Neither <u>Vanessa nor Xiu wants</u> to join the committee.

- If one plural and one singular subject are connected by *or* or *nor*, the verb agrees with the closest subject.

  Neither Vanessa nor <u>the treasurers</u> want to join the committee.

  Neither the treasurers nor <u>Vanessa</u> wants to join the committee.

- In an **inverted sentence**, the subject comes *after* the verb, so the first step is to clearly identify the subject. (Sentences that begin with *there is* and *there are*, for example, as well as questions, are inverted sentences.) Once you correctly identify the subject, then you can make sure your verb agrees. The correct subjects and verbs are underlined.

> Incorrect: *There's plenty of reasons to go.*
>
> Correct: *There <u>are</u> plenty of <u>reasons</u> to go.*
>
> Incorrect: *What's the side effects of this medication?*
>
> Correct: *What <u>are</u> the side <u>effects</u> of this medication?*

Gerunds and Infinitives

Gerunds and **infinitives** have given many students of English a grammar headache, but they are not so difficult to master. Gerunds, as we noted earlier, *look* like verbs because they end in *-ing*, but they actually function as nouns in sentences:

> *Tracy loves <u>camping</u>.*

Here, the "action" Tracy performs is *loves*. The *thing* (noun) she enjoys is *camping*. In the following sentence, however, *camping* is the *action* Tracy performs, so it is functioning as a verb, not as a gerund:

> *Tracy <u>is camping</u> in the Pine Barrens next week.*

Words ending in *-ing* can also function as adjectives:

Some of our <u>camping</u> gear needs to be replaced before our trip.

Here's another example of how the same word can have three different functions:

Verb: *He is <u>screaming</u> loudly.*
Gerund (noun): *That <u>screaming</u> is driving me crazy!*
Adjective: *The <u>screaming</u> boy finally stopped.*

What this means is that you can't count on word endings to determine a word's part of speech. Lots of words that look like verbs may not be. It's how they function in the sentence that counts.

Infinitives are the base (unconjugated) form of the verb preceded by *to*: *to be, to delay, to manage.* They are often part of a verb chain, but they are not the main verb (main action) of a sentence:

Priya likes <u>to write</u> poems.

In this example, *likes* is the main verb; what Priya likes (the action she likes to take) is *to write* poems.

When to Use Infinitives and Gerunds

In many situations, you may be uncertain whether to use an infinitive or a gerund. Which is correct: *I like to swim* or *I like swimming*? In this case, both are correct; *like, hate,* and other verbs that express preference can be followed by either a gerund or infinitive. But other verbs can only be followed by one or the other. Here are a few helpful guidelines:

■ Always use a **gerund** after a preposition.

Keza thought that by taking the train, she would save money and time.

Noriel was afraid of offending her host, but she couldn't eat the dinner.

■ Always use a **gerund** after the following verbs:

admit	dislike	practice
appreciate	enjoy	put off
avoid	escape	quit
can't help	finish	recall
consider	imagine	resist
delay	keep	risk
deny	miss	suggest
discuss	postpone	tolerate

We should discuss <u>buying</u> a new computer.

I am going to quit <u>smoking</u>.

- In general, use an **infinitive** after these verbs:

agree	decide	need	refuse
ask	expect	offer	venture
beg	fail	plan	want
bother	hope	pretend	wish
claim	manage	promise	

> *Aswad promises <u>to be</u> back by noon.*
>
> *Fatima failed <u>to keep</u> her promise.*

- When a noun or pronoun immediately follows these verbs, use an **infinitive**:

advise	expect	require
allow	force	tell
ask	like	urge
cause	need	want
command	order	warn
convince	persuade	
encourage	remind	

> *I'd like you <u>to reconsider</u> my offer.*
>
> *The committee needs you <u>to organize</u> this event.*

Pronouns

Pronouns, as we noted earlier, replace nouns. This keeps us from having to repeat names and objects over and over. But pronouns can be a bit tricky at times. This section reviews the different kinds of pronouns and the rules they follow.

Personal Pronouns

Personal pronouns refer to specific people or things. They can be either singular (*I*) or plural (*we*); they can be subjects (*I*) or objects (*me*).

	SUBJECT	OBJECT
singular	I	me
	you	you
	he	him
	she	her
	it	it
plural	we	us
	they	them

Pronoun mistakes are often made by using the subject form when you really need the object form. Here are two guidelines to follow:

- Always use the object pronoun in a prepositional phrase. **Pronouns and nouns in prepositional phrases are always objects.**

> *He promised to bring a souvenir for Betty and <u>me</u>.*
>
> *Please keep this between <u>us</u>.*

■ Always use the subject pronoun in a *than* construction (comparison). When a pronoun follows *than*, it is usually part of a clause that omits the verb in order not to repeat unnecessarily.

I realize that Alonzo is more talented than I. [than I am]

Sandra is much more reliable than he. [than he is]

Indefinite Pronouns

Unlike personal pronouns, **indefinite pronouns**, such as *anybody* and *everyone*, don't refer to a specific person. The following indefinite pronouns are **always singular** and require singular verbs:

anyone, anybody	everyone, everybody
no one, nobody	someone, somebody
either, neither	each
one	

Everybody has a chance to win.
Neither child admits to eating the cookies.
Has anyone seen my keys?

The following indefinite pronouns are **always plural**:

both few many several

Both sound like good options.
Only a few are left.

These indefinite pronouns can be singular or plural, depending upon the noun or pronoun to which they refer:

all any most none some

Some of the money is counterfeit.
Some of the coins are valuable.
None of the animals have been fed.
All of the bread is moldy.

Pronoun-Antecedent Agreement

Just as subjects (both nouns and pronouns) must agree with their verbs, pronouns must also agree with their **antecedents**—the words they replace. For example:

Children will often believe everything their parents tell them.

The word *children* is the antecedent and is replaced by *their* and *them* in the sentence. Because *children* is plural, the pronouns must also be plural.

Indefinite pronouns can also be antecedents. Singular indefinite pronouns require singular pronouns:

Everyone has his or her own reasons for coming.
Neither of the physicists could explain what she saw.

A BAD HABIT

One of the most common mistakes we make when speaking and writing is an error of pronoun-antecedent agreement. We often say sentences like the following:

Did everyone bring their notebooks?

Most people make this mistake because it's easier (shorter and faster) to say their—but it's not correct. When the antecedent is singular, the pronouns must be singular, too:

Did everyone bring his or her notebook?

Plural indefinite pronouns, on the other hand, require plural pronouns, just like they need plural verbs:

both   few   many   several

<u>Both</u> of them have finished <u>their</u> work.
Only a <u>few</u> are still in <u>their</u> original cases.

Finally, those pronouns that can be either singular or plural, depending upon the noun or pronoun to which they refer, should take the pronoun that matches their referent. If the antecedent is singular, the pronoun and verb must also be singular. If the antecedent is plural, they must be plural:

all   any   most   none   some

All of the chocolate is gone. It was delicious!
All of the cookies are gone. They were delicious!

None of the information is accurate; it's all out of date.
None of the facts are accurate; they are all out of date.

Pronoun Consistency

Just as you need to be consistent in verb tense, you should also be consistent in your pronoun *point of view*. Pronouns can be:

	SINGULAR	PLURAL
First person	I, me	we, us, our
Second person	you	you (all)
Third person	he, she, it	they, them, their
	one	

A passage that begins in the third-person plural should continue to use that third-person plural point of view.

Incorrect:	*We have tested our hypothesis and the team believes it is correct.*
Correct:	*We have tested our hypothesis and we believe it is correct.*

Incorrect:	*If you prepare carefully, one can expect to pass the exam.*
Correct:	*If you prepare carefully, you can expect to pass the exam.* OR *If one prepares carefully, one can expect to pass the exam.*

Possessive Pronouns

The **possessive pronouns** *its*, *your*, *their*, and *whose* are often confused with the contractions *it's* (*it is* or *it has*), *you're* (*you are*), *they're* (*they are*), and *who's* (*who is*). Because we use apostrophes to show possession in nouns (*Louise's* truck, the *rug's* pattern), many people make the mistake of thinking that pronouns use apostrophes for possession, too. But possessive pronouns *do not* take apostrophes. When a pronoun has an apostrophe, it always shows **contraction**.

POSSESIVE PRONOUN	MEANING	EXAMPLE
its	belonging to it	*The dog chased its tail.*
your	belonging to you	*Your time is up.*
their	belonging to them	*Their words were comforting.*
whose	belonging to who	*Whose tickets are these?*

CONTRACTIONS		
it's	it is	*It's time to eat.*
you're	you are	*You're not going to believe your eyes.*
they're	they are	*They're getting their tickets now.*
who's	who has who is	*Who's got my tickets?* *Who's sitting in front?*

The pronouns *who, that,* and *which* are also often confused. Here are the general guidelines for using these pronouns correctly:

- Use **who** or **whom** when referring to people:

  She is the one who should make that decision, not me.

- Use **that** when referring to things:

  This is the most important decision that she will make as director.

- Use **which** when introducing clauses that are not essential to the information in the sentence, unless they refer to people. In that case, use **who**.

  Emily married Sonny, who has been in love with her since first grade.

  Antoinette, who is a computer programmer, would be a good match for Daniel.

The film, which is a comedy, won several awards.

Adjectives and Adverbs

Adjectives and adverbs help give our sentences color; they describe things and actions. **Adjectives** describe nouns and pronouns and tell us *which one, what kind,* and *how many.* See the following table.

WHICH ONE?	WHAT KIND?	HOW MANY?
that book	*romance* novel	*several* chapters
the *other* class	*sleep* expense	*multiple* choices
the *last* song	*jazzy* melody	*six* awards

Adverbs, on the other hand, describe verbs, adjectives, and other adverbs. They tell us *where, when, how,* and *to what extent.* See the following table.

WHERE?	WHEN?	HOW?	TO WHAT EXTENT?
The plane flew *south.*	Jude arrived *early.*	She sang *beautifully.*	Anthony is *very* talented.
Put the chair *here.*	She registered *late.*	The system is behaving *erratically.*	Eleanor is still *extremely* ill.

Remember to keep modifiers as close as possible to what they modify.

Fewer/Less, Number/Amount

As a rule, use the adjective *fewer* to modify plural nouns or things that can be counted. Use *less* for singular nouns that represent a quantity or a degree. Most nouns to which an *-s* can be added require the adjective *fewer*.

> Use <u>less salt</u> this time.　　Use <u>fewer eggs</u> this time.
>
> I had <u>less reason</u> to go this time.　　I had <u>fewer reasons</u> to go this time.

Good/Bad, Well/Badly

These pairs of words—*good/well, bad/badly*—are often confused. The key to proper usage is to understand their function in the sentence. *Good* and *bad* are adjectives; they should be used to modify only nouns and pronouns. *Well* and *badly* are adverbs; they should be used to modify verbs.

> I was surprised by how <u>good</u> Sebastian's <u>cake</u> was.
>
> Jennelle hasn't been <u>feeling well</u> lately.
>
> Her <u>attitude</u> is <u>good</u>, but she didn't <u>do well</u> in the interview.

Comparisons

An important function of adjectives and adverbs is comparisons. When you are comparing *two* things, use the **comparative form** (*-er*) of the modifier. If you are comparing more than two things, use the **superlative form** (*-est*) of the modifier.

To create the **comparative** form, either:

1. add *-er* to the modifier OR
2. place the word *more* or *less* before the modifier.

In general, add *-er* to short modifiers (one or two syllables). Use *more* or *less* with modifiers of more than two syllables.

> cheaper　　less expensive
>
> smarter　　more intelligent

To create the **superlative** form, either:

1. add *-est* to the modifier OR
2. place the word *most* or *least* before the modifier.

Again, as a general rule, add *-est* to short modifiers (one or two syllables). Use *most* or *least* with modifiers that are more than two syllables.

> Wanda is <u>more experienced</u> than I, but I am the <u>most familiar</u> with the software.
>
> Ahmed is clearly the <u>smartest</u> student in the class.

Double Comparisons and Double Negatives

Be sure to avoid **double comparisons**. Don't use both *-er/-est* and *more/less* or *most/least* together.

> <u>Incorrect</u>: She has the <u>most longest</u> hair I've ever seen.
> <u>Correct</u>: She has the <u>longest</u> hair I've ever seen.
>
> <u>Incorrect</u>: Minsun is <u>more happier</u> now.
> <u>Correct</u>: Minsun is <u>happier</u> now.

Likewise, be sure to avoid **double negatives**. When a negative word such as *no* or *not* is added to a statement that is already negative, a double negative—and potential confusion—results. *Hardly* and *barely* are also negative words. Remember, one negative is all you need.

> <u>Incorrect</u>: He doesn't have no idea what she's talking about.
> <u>Correct</u>: He does<u>n't</u> have any idea what she's talking about.
> He has <u>no</u> idea what she's talking about.
>
> <u>Incorrect</u>: I can't hardly wait to see you.
> <u>Correct</u>: I can <u>hardly</u> wait to see you.
> I ca<u>n't</u> wait to see you.

Prepositional Idioms

Another aspect of usage is prepositional idioms: the specific word/preposition combinations that we use in the English language, such as *take care of* and *according to*.

What follows is a list of some of the most common prepositional idioms. Review the list carefully to be sure you are using prepositional idioms correctly.

according to	concerned with	in accordance with	regard to
afraid of	congratulate on	incapable of	related to
anxious about	conscious of	in conflict	rely on/upon
apologize for (something)	consist of	inferior to	respect for
approve of	equal to	in the habit of	satisfied with
ashamed of	except for	in the near future	similar to
aware of	fond of	interested in	sorry for
blame (someone) for (something)	from now on	knowledge of	suspicious of
bored with	from time to time	next to	take care of
capable of	frown on/upon	of the opinion	thank (someone) for (something)
compete with	full of	on top of	tired of
complain about	glance at (something)/ glance through (something, e.g., a book)	opposite of	with regard to
composed of	grateful to (someone)	prior to	
concentrate on	grateful for (something)	proud of	

Mechanics

Mechanics refers to the rules that govern punctuation marks, capitalization, and spelling. Like the rules that govern usage, the rules that govern sentence mechanics help us keep our sentences and their meanings clear.

Punctuation

Punctuation marks are the symbols used to separate sentences, express emotions, and show relationships between objects and ideas. Correct punctuation makes your meaning clear and adds drama and style to your sentences. Poor punctuation, on the other hand, can lead to a great deal of confusion for your readers and can send a message other than the one you intended. For example, take a look at the following two versions of the same sentence:

> *Don't bother Xavier.*
> *Don't bother, Xavier.*

These sentences use the same words, but have very different meanings because of punctuation. In the first sentence, the comma indicates that the speaker is telling *the reader* not to bother Xavier. In the second sentence, the speaker is telling *Xavier* not to bother. Here's another example of how punctuation can drastically affect meaning:

> *You should eat Zak so you can think clearly during your interview.*

Because this sentence is missing some essential punctuation, the sentence says something very different from what the author intended. The speaker isn't telling *the reader* to eat *Zak*; rather, she's telling *Zak* to eat. The sentence should be revised as follows:

> *You should eat, Zak, so you can think clearly during your interview.*

Punctuation helps to create meaning, and it also has another important function: It enables writers to express a variety of tones and emotions. For example, take a look at these two versions of the same sentence:

> *Wait—I'm coming with you!*
> *Wait, I'm coming with you.*

The first sentence clearly expresses more urgency and excitement thanks to the dash and exclamation point. The second sentence, with its comma and period, does not express emotion; the sentence is neutral.

Punctuation Guidelines

There are many rules for punctuation, and the better you know them, the more correctly and effectively you can punctuate your sentences. The following table lists the main punctuation marks and guidelines for when to use them:

YOUR PURPOSE:	USE THIS PUNCTUATION:	EXAMPLE:
End a sentence	**period [.]**	Most sentences end in a period.
Connect complete sentences *(two independent clauses)*	**semicolon [;]**	*A semicolon can connect two sentences; it is an excellent way to show that two ideas are related.*
	comma [,] *and a conjunction [and, or, nor, for, so, but, yet]*	*Leslie is coming, but Huang is staying home.*
	dash [—] (less common, but more dramatic)	*Hurry up—we're late!*
Connect items in a list	**comma [,]** but if one or more items in that list already have a comma, use a **semicolon [;]**	*His odd shopping list included batteries, a box of envelopes, and a can of spam.*
		The castaways included a professor, who was the group's leader; an actress; and a millionaire and his wife.
Introduce a list of three or more items	**colon [:]**	*There are three things I want to do before I die: go on a cruise, go skydiving, and surf.*
		Colons have three functions: introducing long lists, introducing quotations, and introducing explanations.
Introduce an explanation (what follows "explains" or "answers" what precedes)	**colon [:]**	*You know what they say about real estate: Location is everything.*
Introduce a quotation (words directly spoken)	**colon [:]** or **comma [,]**	*She yelled, "Let's get out of here!"*
Indicate a quotation	**quotation marks [" "]**	*"To be or not to be?" is one of the most famous lines from Hamlet.*

Indicate a question	**question mark [?]**	*What time is it?*
		"How much longer?" he asked.
Connect two words that work together as one object or modifier	**hyphen [-]**	*Mother-in-law, turn-of-the-century poet, French-fried potatoes*
Separate a word or phrase for emphasis	**dash [—]**	*Never lie—never.*
		We're late—very late!
Separate a word or phrase that is relevant but not essential information	**commas [,]**	*Elaine, my roommate, is from Chicago.*
		Her nickname as a child, her mother told me, was "Boo-boo."
Separate a word or phrase that is relevant but secondary information	**parentheses [( )]**	*There is an exception to every rule (including this one).*
Show possession or contraction	**apostrophe [']**	*Why is Lisa's wallet in Ben's backpack?*

Comma Rules

Many mechanics questions will deal with commas, the most common punctuation mark within sentences. The presence and placement of commas can dramatically affect meaning and can make the difference between clarity and confusion. The previous chart lists four comma uses, but there are several others. What follows is a complete list of comma rules. If you know them, then you can be sure your sentences are clear. You will also be able to tell whether or not a comma is needed to correct a sentence.

Use a comma:

1. with a coordinating conjunction to separate two complete sentences. Note that a comma is *not* required if both parts of the sentence are four words or less.

   Let's eat first, and then we will go to a movie.

   I'm definitely older, but I don't think I'm much wiser.

   I love him and he loves me.

2. to set off introductory words, phrases, or clauses.

   Next year, I will stick to my New Year's resolutions.

   Wow, that sure looks good!

   Because the game was canceled, Jane took the kids bowling.

3. to set off a direct address, interjection, or transitional phrase.

   Well, Jeb, it looks like we will be stuck here for a while.

   His hair color is a little, um, unusual.

   My heavens, this is spicy chili!

   Sea horses, for example, are unusual in that the males carry the eggs.

4. between two modifiers that could be replaced by *and*.

> *He is a mean, contemptible person.*
> (Both *mean* and *contemptible* modify *person*.)

> Incorrect: *Denny's old, stamp collection is priceless.*
> Correct: *Denny's old stamp collection is priceless.*
> (You cannot put "and" between *old* and *stamp*; *old* describes *stamp* and *stamp* modifies *collection*. They do not modify the same noun.)

5. to set off information that is relevant but not essential (nonrestrictive).

> Essential, not set off:
> *The woman <u>who wrote</u> Happy Moon is coming to our local bookstore.*
> (We need this information to know which woman we're talking about.)

> Nonessential, set off by commas:
> *The dog, lost and confused, wandered into the street.*
> (The fact that the dog was lost and confused is not essential to the sentence.)

> Essential, not set off:
> *Witnesses <u>who lie under oath</u> will be prosecuted.*

> Nonessential, set off by commas:
> *Leeland, who at first refused to testify, later admitted to lying under oath.*

6. to separate items in a series.

> *The price for the cruise includes breakfast, lunch, dinner, and entertainment.*

> *The recipe calls for fresh cilantro, chopped onions, diced tomatoes, and lemon juice.*

7. to set off most quotations. As a general rule, short quotations are introduced by commas while long quotations (several sentences or more) are introduced by colons. All speech in dialogue should be set off by commas.

> *"Let's get going," he said impatiently.*

> *Rene Descartes is famous for the words, "I think, therefore I am."*

> *Joseph said, "Please forgive me for jumping to conclusions."*

8. to set off parts of dates, numbers, titles, and addresses.

> *She was born on April 30, 2002.*

> *Please print 3,000 copies.*

> *Tiberio Mendola, MD, is my new doctor.*

> *Please deliver the package to me at 30 Willow Road, Trenton, NJ.*

9. to prevent confusion, as in cases when a word is repeated.

> *What it is, is a big mistake.*

> *After I, comes J.*

Capitalization

Capitalization is an important tool to help us identify (1) the beginning of a new sentence and (2) proper nouns and adjectives. Here are six rules for correct capitalization:

1. Capitalize the first word of a sentence.

   Please close the door.

   What are you trying to say?

   If you are quoting a full sentence within your own sentence, use a capital letter, unless you introduce the quote with *that*.

   The author notes, "A shocking three out of four students admitted to cheating."

   The author notes that "a shocking three out of four students admitted to cheating."

   If you have a full sentence within parentheses, that sentence should be capitalized as well (and the end punctuation mark should be within the parentheses).

   He was expelled for repeatedly violating the school's code of conduct (including several instances of stealing and cheating).

   He was expelled for repeatedly violating the school's code of conduct. (He was caught stealing and cheating several times.)

2. Capitalize proper nouns. A **proper noun** is the name of a specific person, place, or thing (as opposed to a *general* person, place, or thing). See the following table.

3. Capitalize the days of the week and months of the year, but not the seasons.

   It was a warm spring day in May.

   Wednesday is the first official day of autumn.

4. Capitalize the names of countries, nationalities, geographical regions, languages, and religions.

   He has traveled to Brazil and Tunisia.

   She is half Chinese, half French.

   She is from the South.
   (But, *Drive south for five miles.*)

   We speak Spanish at home.

   He is a devout Catholic.

5. Capitalize titles that come *before* proper names.

Judge Lydia Ng	*Lydia Ng, judge in the Fifth District*
Professor Lee Chang	*Lee Chang, professor of physical science*
Vice President Tilda Stanton	*Tilda Stanton, vice president*

6. Capitalize titles of **publications**, including books, stories, poems, plays, articles, speeches, essays, and other documents, and **works of art**, including films, paintings, and musical compositions.

   Pablo Picasso's painting Guernica *captures the agony of the Spanish Civil War.*

   Read Susan Sontag's essay "On Photography" for class tomorrow.

   The Declaration of Independence is a sacred document.

CAPITALIZE (SPECIFIC)	DON'T CAPITALIZE (GENERAL)
Jennifer Johnson (specific person)	the lady
Algebra 101 (specific class)	my math class
Main Street (specific street)	on the street
Frosted Flakes (specific brand)	good cereal
Caspian Sea (specific sea)	deep sea/ocean
Lincoln Memorial (specific monument)	impressive memorial/monument
USS Cole (specific ship)	naval destroyer
Dade High School (specific school)	our high school
Precambrian Age (specific time period)	long ago
Microsoft Corporation (specific company)	that company

Spelling

Homonyms, contractions, and possessives are an important part of basic grammar. The spelling of these words is reviewed in the following section.

Contractions and Possessives

Confusion between contractions and possessives results in some of the most common spelling mistakes.

Contractions are words that use an apostrophe to show that a letter or letters have been omitted from the word(s). **Possessive pronouns** indicate ownership of objects and ideas. They DO NOT take an apostrophe.

POSSESSIVE PRONOUN	MEANING	EXAMPLE
its	belonging to it	The dog chased its tail.
your	belonging to you	Your time is up.
their	belonging to them	Their words were comforting.
whose	belonging to who	Whose tickets are these?

CONTRACTION	MEANING	EXAMPLE
it's	it is	It's time to eat.
you're	you are	You're not going to believe your eyes.
they're	they are	They're getting their tickets now.
who's	who is, who has	Who's got my tickets?

Homonyms

Homonyms are words that sound alike but have different spellings and meanings. Here are some of the most common homonyms:

accept	to take or receive
except	leave out
affect	(*verb*) to have an influence
effect	(*noun*) the result or impact of something
all ready	fully prepared
already	previously
bare	(*adj*) uncovered; (*verb*) to uncover
bear	(*noun*) animal; (*verb*) to carry or endure
brake	(*verb*) to stop; (*noun*) device for stopping
break	(*verb*) to fracture or rend; (*noun*) a pause or temporary stoppage
buy	(*verb*) to purchase
by	(*preposition*) next to or near; through
desert	(*noun*) dry area; (*verb*) to abandon
dessert	sweet course at the end of a meal
every day	each day
everyday	ordinary; daily
hear	(*verb*) to perceive with the ears
here	(*adverb*) in this place
know	to understand, be aware of
no	negative—opposite of yes
loose	(*adj*) not tight; not confined
lose	(*verb*) to misplace; to fail to win
may be	might be (possibility)
maybe	perhaps
morning	the first part of the day
mourning	grieving
passed	past tense of pass (to go by)
past	beyond; events that have already occurred
patience	quality of being patient; able to wait
patients	people under medical care
personal	(*adj*) private or pertaining to the individual
personnel	(*noun*) employees

presence	condition of being
presents	gifts
principal	most important; head of a school
principle	fundamental truth
right	correct; opposite of left
rite	ceremony
write	produce words on a surface
scene	setting or view
seen	past participle of see
than	used to compare (*he is taller than I*)
then	at that time, therefore (*first this, then that; if you think it's good, then I'll do it*)
their	possessive form of *they*
there	location; in that place
through	in one side and out the other; by means of
threw	past tense of *throw*
to	(*preposition*) in the direction of
too	(*adverb*) in addition; excessive
two	number
waist	part of the body
waste	(*verb*) to squander; (*noun*) trash
weak	feeble
week	seven days
weather	climatic conditions
whether	introducing a choice
which	what, that
witch	practitioner of witchcraft

GLOSSARY

alliteration: beginning all important words with the same letter; example: "Peter Piper picked a peck of pickled peppers," where all important words begin with *p*

anecdote: a short story used to illustrate some principle, frequently drawn from personal experience

attention span: the average length of time that your audience will be paying close attention to your words; in general, most people will listen attentively for approximately three minutes

audience: any person or group that is listening to you speak

body: the major portion of your speech in which you expound on your topic in detail

citation: details on where you found certain information. Correct citation for printed material (books, magazines, etc.) will include author, title of book (or magazine, journal, etc.), publisher's name and location, copyright date, and page number.

cliché: a phrase or common expression that is over used and trite; examples: "think outside the box"; "all's well that ends well"; "been there, done that"

conclusion: the final portion of your speech in which you conclude your talk and help your audience draw conclusions from what you've said

demonstrative speech: a presentation that *demonstrates*, or explains how to do something

enunciate: to clearly speak each syllable in a word, rather than slurring them together

environment: the tangible and intangible factors involved in the setting of your speech—seating, mechanical devices, external noise, etc.

ethos: a speaker's credibility; more accurately, the audience's *perception* of whether or not the speaker is reliable

etiquette: common rules of courtesy; good manners

eulogy: literally "good word"; a memorial speech given in honor of a deceased person

eye contact: looking into the eyes of an individual in the audience, holding the gaze for approximately five seconds

flip charts: large pads of oversized paper supported by an easel

grooming: making your physical appearance appropriate to your speech. Dress one notch better than your audience: If they're in casual attire, you should be dressed to business casual, and so forth. *See Lesson 13.*

honorarium: a speech honoring someone; a financial gift given to a speaker after a speech

illustrations: stories, examples, or anecdotes that provide a practical application of one of your ideas or points; taking an abstract idea and making it concrete with real-life application

informative speech: a presentation designed to *inform* or teach the audience some general information

introduction: the opening portion of your speech in which you introduce yourself, your topic, your goal, and how you'll achieve your goal

logos: words, concepts, and logic used to build a persuasive speech

metaphor: a comparison between two things that are not clearly related. "My love is a rose" is a metaphor. Metaphors and similes must be explained to be effective, however: "My love is a rose, opening to the sunshine of your smile."

object lesson: a presentation that uses three-dimensional objects that illustrate the topic or sub-points in some way

opening out: the technique of facing the audience squarely, without placing your arms or any objects between you and them. An opened-out posture is upright, shoulders squared, chin up, eyes on the audience, hands and arms at the sides or moving in gestures.

outline: a rough overview of what you'll say at each point in your speech. An outline should include your introduction, body, and conclusion and should contain only *notes* on what you'll say, not the exact wording.

overhead projector: a mechanical device that illuminates a clear sheet of acetate, called an *overhead transparency*, and projects the image on a screen

overhead transparency: a clear sheet of acetate with words or pictures printed or drawn onto it, projected on a screen

pathos: emotional appeals used to persuade an audience

persuasive speech: a presentation that attempts to *persuade* the audience to hold a certain opinion

plagiarism: quoting someone else's words, or using someone else's materials, without giving due credit. This is illegal, as well as unethical.

PowerPoint: a computer software program used to create digital images of charts, graphs, bulleted lists, text, etc., intended to be projected on a screen

public speaking: communicating orally (speaking) to two or more people at one time

repetition: using a word or phrase in each major point of your speech to make them memorable, such as *Paint Techniques*, *Paint Selection*, and *Paint Application*

rhetoric: the art of using words to persuade

rhetorical devices: techniques used to make your speech more convincing or memorable, such as metaphor, alliteration, poetry, etc.

sequence: naming all your sub-points in alphabetical or numerical order, such as *Antiseptic Qualities*, *Breath Cleansing*, and *Cost*

setting: the physical location where you will give your speech

simile: a comparison between two things using *like* or *as*. "My love is like a rose" is a simile, because it says that your love is *similar* to (like) a rose. Metaphors and similes must be explained to be effective, however: "My love is like a rose when its fragrance breathes sweetness into my dark days."

speech: a prepared presentation intended to be spoken before an audience

speed bumps: verbal techniques that command your audience's attention, such as an unexpected pause, dramatic gestures, command phrase ("Now pay attention to this"), etc.

spice: any element that helps the audience pay attention to your words, such as humor, visual aids, gestures, motion, etc.

stage fright: the feeling of anxiety or nervousness that comes over a person prior to speaking in front of an audience

thesis: an opinion you intend to prove as true in your speech. Note that a thesis must be proven; if you can't prove it's true, you will not persuade your audience.

TMI: "too much information"; the condition of an audience being overloaded with too many facts, figures, statistics, etc.

tone: the emotional attitude established by your speech, by the audience's response, or by your delivery

topic: what your speech is about; the subject matter

upspeak: the tendency to use an upward inflection in sentences or phrases, making them sound like a question rather than a statement

visual aids: anything that you can visually show to the audience that will help them to understand your topic or ideas

NOTES

NOTES

NOTES

NOTES

NOTES

NOTES

NOTES

NOTES

NOTES

NOTES